Leadership in Managing Facilities

A ONE-YEAR JOURNEY

by Richard P. Payant, DBA, CFM, CPE

Dorrance Publishing Co
585 Alpha Drive
Suite 103
Pittsburgh, PA 15238
Visit our website at *www.dorrancebookstore.com*

ISBN: 979-8-88729-391-2
eISBN: 979-8-88729-891-7

Leadership in Managing Facilities
A ONE-YEAR JOURNEY

BOOK REVIEWS

Reading in the first person has a pleasing uniqueness that hammers home the core principles of Facilities Management. Effective communication, listening skills, and developing relationships have never been easier to understand. People are Facilities and Facilities are people. This book is a great companion to any typical Facilities Management Guide.

James C.

I found it to be an easy reading eye-opening journey through what goes on behind the scenes in the world of a Facilities Management Director. The book is relatable and illuminates details of many situations and challenges to be encountered and the processes followed to achieve successful outcomes. It also makes clear the benefits of having the right team in place from top to bottom, people who have their heads in the game, and a genuine concern for the facility in their hearts.

I enjoyed relating to the various characters, and better understanding their roles.

Thomas C.

I like the "first-person format" and it's much more engaging than a textbook style read.

Marc S.

Great read!

The book is well organized and the idea of placing the reader in mock real-life scenarios is creative and entertaining.

The book is a treasure trove of how to organize, communicate at all levels, plan, and prepare.

The book makes for enjoyable reading but more importantly can prepare new FM managers for real-life challenges along the entire spectrum of effective approaches to leading and managing.

This book can also benefit future leaders in FM as they start their journey in the world of facility management..

Randy S.

DEDICATION

To my family, Gayle, Nicole, Chris, Michelle, and Danielle who encouraged me to continue writing and having the book published. They never doubted.

To all the facility management employees I was fortunate to get to know and who always supported what we were doing.

To a special friend, my source of inspiration, with much gratitude.

ACKNOWLEDGMENTS

The experiences I amassed in the profession of facility management are based on challenges and interactions with people with whom I worked or with whom I associated throughout the years. All these people helped me grow, learn, and expand my understanding of FM. This book would not have been completed without their valued support. It is my pleasure to express my appreciation for all they have done.

The time I spent in the military was an opportunity to work for and with many talented leaders who taught me what it means to be a leader and manager, and what a facility manager must do to be successful. To them, I am forever grateful. I want to express my sincere thanks to the following individuals: Maj. Gen. William McGrath, Maj. Gen. Peter Offringa, Col. Robert Ayers, Lt Col. Vincent Parmesano, Bryan Nix, Randy Sinkler, Arthur Weissmuller, Ralph Mench, Jim Medbourne, and Ed Miechionchek. Without their help, I would not have gained the experience needed to be successful in managing facilities.

Upon leaving the Army, I was selected to be the Director of Facilities Management at a major university. Karen Frank encouraged me to persevere and provided tips to carefully navigate the many complex issues and personalities in facilities management. Coral Harris guided and educated me on human resource policies. Isaac Blair coached me on the intricacies of managing renovation, new construction projects, and quality assurance. Don Phillip helped me better understand contract law and gave me many ideas on partnering with contractors and vendors. Marianne Green, my administrative assistant, is the one who developed the policy and procedures format and kept all of them up-dated. Marianne also managed the department newsletter, and the birthday and sympathy card wishes. Her help was greatly appreciated.

My sincere thanks also go to the managers who supported me and made good recommendations on how to improve operations and maintenance: David Capp, Paul Murphy, Steve Sakach, Mike Pontti, James Connor, Marc Smith, Bill Del Vecchio, Juan Madrid, Mike Morse, Ian Lewis, Craig Day, Pat Hughes, John Ortiz, Mohammed Nosair, Greg Burton, Alvin Brown, and Thomas Crowley.

With much gratitude, I also want to single out other individuals who helped me on my journey. Dr. Bernard (Barney) Lewis, a true friend, published more than 20 books on facility management and eventually convinced me to write. Sherman Sawhney, a good friend, and an engineering consultant provided valuable advice on managing the vehicle fleet and automotive garage operations.

Dave Cotts, former Chief Facilities Officer at the World Bank, convinced me to teach FM courses. After three requests, I conceded and have been teaching for more than 20 years. Dave also was the author of the first and second editions of *The Facility Management Handbook*. He asked me to be a co-author of the third edition. Dave is a friend who has done much for the FM profession and for me.

Our youngest daughter Danielle provided recommendations and edits to the first draft. Our middle daughter Michelle continually encouraged me to pursue publication. Our son Chris, a public works director based in Massachusetts, reviewed the first draft and convinced me to keep going. Our oldest daughter, Nicole, also enthusiastically supported the endeavor.

Robert Weinstein, who edited this book, patiently answered all my questions and provided recommendations and improvements on making the book more readable. I truly enjoyed working with him and highly recommend him for future endeavors such as this.

All of the individuals above were instrumental in my obtaining the experiences needed to be successful in the facility management profession. However, the one individual who inspired me the most is my wife, Gayle. She encouraged me to write about my experiences. Her continual support kept me striving to achieve my goal. She believed in me, and this book is the result.

TABLE OF CONTENTS

Foreword xiii

Preface xv

Introduction xix

Part I: First Week Plan

Chapter 1: New Job 3

Chapter 2: First Day 5

Chapter 3: First Week Meetings 11

Part I Discussion Questions 15

Part II: The First Six Months

Chapter 4: Learning Everything 19

Chapter 5: Department Issues 21

Chapter 6: Manage By Walking Around 23

Chapter 7: Policies and Procedures 27

Chapter 8: Training 31

Chapter 9: Culture and Perception 37

Chapter 10: Asset Management and Preventive Maintenance 41

Chapter 11: Automation 47

Chapter 12: Procurement and Contracting 53

Chapter 13: Emergency Management Plan 57

Chapter 14: Measuring 67

Chapter 15: Design and Engineering 71

Chapter 16: Sustainability 75

Chapter 17: Monthly Updates. 79
Part II Discussion Questions. 82

Part III: The First Year

Chapter 18: A Decision. 85
Chapter 19: Facility Management Strategy 89
Chapter 20: Change Management 93
Chapter 21: Vision, Mission, Goals 97
Chapter 22: The Plan. 101
Chapter 23: Quality Management and Customer Service 105
Chapter 24: Planning and Budgeting. 109
Chapter 25: Fire Protection. 115
Chapter 26: Indoor Air Quality 119
Chapter 27: Workplace Violence. 125
Chapter 28: Annual Report 129
Chapter 29: Change with the Times. 133
Chapter 30: First Year Update. 139
Chapter 31: The Final Chapter. 141
Part III Discussion Questions. 144

Appendices

A: Philosophy and Style 149
B: Facility Management Policies and Procedures 151
C: Vision, Mission, Goals. 157

References. **163**
Index. **165**
About the Author. **183**

FOREWORD

Rich Payant is a master facility manager and an extraordinary Facilities Management (FM) trainer. I've had the pleasure of being a student of Rich in my past life as the director of the facilities department for one of the largest public school systems in America, and I've tapped him to train my managers and supervisors in my current position as the director of operations at a fast-growing public university. His new book, "Leadership in Managing Facilities: A One-Year Journey," covers all the wide-ranging topics and situations a facility manager encounters and is an excellent addition to any FM's library. It will be a "go-to" resource for me.

Of personal interest, because of their timeliness, are his expertise in quality customer service, sustainability, and indoor air quality. Today's facility occupants and users are informed. They demand facilities that are safe, comfortable, and promote good health, while also wanting to know their facilities are built and maintained in a manner that embraces sustainable practices. Rich does an outstanding job illustrating how organization leadership and stakeholders can both be demanding in these areas, and it's the FM's task to determine how to address these issues with limited budgets and personnel resources.

I especially enjoyed how Rich uses characters to allow us to journey through the life of a facility manager and meet all the people facility managers encounter, interact with, and report to on a daily basis. Ultimately, the success of facility managers hangs on their ability to communicate, inspire, motivate, demonstrate empathy, build trust, and be respectful toward everyone with whom they associate. Facility managers have to understand and be able to work with the higher organization leadership, stakeholders, colleagues, employees, parents, and students.

Anyone working in facility management or desiring to advance themselves in this profession should read this book. It contains useful examples and tips, based on actual experiences, no matter what level you are at. This book will be a great companion book to all the more technical FM books in your personal library. If you want to be successful in this profession —-Read this book!

Steve Vollmer
Director of Facility Operations
George Mason University

PREFACE

Teaching Facility Management (FM) courses for over 20 years has given me the opportunity to know and educate almost 1,000 FM students. I've taught courses on basic principles of FM, communications, leadership, quality management and customer service, operations and maintenance, and emergency management for FM. This book has given me the opportunity to write my thoughts and experiences. Listening to students in my classes and reading various articles and blogs, I found the same questions were asked repeatedly by people wanting to advance themselves. How do I get ahead? What Facility Management or other professional certifications do I need? Where can I get information on the FM profession?

There are many professional books available for aspiring facility managers and property managers to find information. Most of them are traditional textbooks, guidebooks, and books with checklists. Some are technical in nature or provide general information and some are inspiring. However, none tell how to manage facilities or properties in a story form that captures the reader's interest and simultaneously educates them on techniques, tips, and skills needed for success. This book is intended to be a companion book for all facility management books—especially for *The Facility Management Handbook*, *Facility Manager's Maintenance Handbook*, and *Emergency Management for Facility and Property Managers*.

A novice to this profession should first ask: What is Facility Management? Understanding the complex role of facility management and property management means developing an awareness of today's smart technology and realizing many organizations now work 24/7/365. Consequently, the complexity and pace of maintaining and operating facilities have dramatically increased. Many facilities have data centers that must operate continuously and cannot afford disruptions. Downtime costs money, sometimes millions of dollars per hour.

Anyone working in facility, property management, and public works should recognize that the physical plant must operate safely, efficiently, be capable of adapting to changing situations, and operate in a cost-effective manner so the supported organization (the International Facility Management Association uses the term *demand organization*) can be effective at what it does. This may sound simple to do. But to operate and maintain facilities, the facility manager is responsible to ensure the facilities meet health, safety, and legal requirements. Life safety and property protection are always the number one and two goals.

Some of the areas in which larger facility organizations oversee and become involved will include the following:

- Space management,
- Office relocations,
- Coordinating and overseeing renovations and building upgrade projects,
- Strategic and tactical planning of operations and maintenance,
- Master planning,
- Meeting compliance with building codes and government regulations,
- Day-to-day building maintenance and cleaning,
- Managing budgets,
- Transportation and parking,
- Grounds and landscape management,
- Physical security,
- Energy management,
- Solid waste and recycling,
- Sustainability, and
- Managing emergencies.

Managing facilities and properties is challenging and demanding. There is always a need for resources, which are often difficult to obtain. Acquiring resources requires funding, be it for emergencies, projects, or people. To be successful in these professions, you must be tenacious and passionate because these professions are demanding.

The clients, customers, citizens, tenants, faculty members, researchers, parents, visitors, and students frequently require support from the facility management department. People need electricity, potable water, sanitary systems, air conditioning and heat, and building conveyance systems. They expect clean buildings, clean restrooms, manicured grounds, trash (solid waste) collected (and some of it recycled), security lock systems, and parking lots and streets maintained and free of snow and debris.

People who work in the facility and property management business, as well as public works, must be communicators and capable of building good relationships with a diverse group of vendors, contractors, architects and engineers, employees, tenants, citizens, customers, parents, students, faculty members, and executives. These individuals need to be adept at developing budgets, understanding technology, and solving problems. They need to be capable of multitasking, training, motivating employees, managing emergencies, focusing on quality management, and providing great customer service.

This book is written to spotlight the work of facility managers and property managers, as well as some public works directors. It also describes the challenges and emergencies they encounter almost daily. The focus is on a facility manager's first year in the position. The book is written in story form to make it easier and more interesting for the reader to understand and associate with the daily demands. The diverse FM storyline presented applies to a fictional university that could be located anywhere. However, its application is relevant to all FM organizations worldwide. All the situations and examples are actual experiences. As you read, you will find many subtle tips on how to be successful—not just as a facility and property manager, or public works director, but also as a leader and manager.

The key takeaways of this book are:

- **Communication.** The *way* we communicate and *how* we communicate to be successful is critical in the facilities management profession.
- **Leadership and management.** Leadership is based on your position and authority to influence the organization's direction and to inspire

and motivate desired behavior. Management involves getting things done through planning, organizing, directing, controlling, and budgeting. To be an effective facility manager, you must be both a leader *and* a manager.

- **Respect for all people.** Treat everyone with respect and in a firm and fair way. Help people wherever possible. In any organization, there are always the "ten percenters." These are the folks who constantly challenge you. Somehow you have to look beyond them; otherwise, you could spend most of your time trying to change them or discipline them.
- **Maintain a positive attitude.** Stay focused! It's easy to get overwhelmed, angry, and remain negative. The hard thing to do is be positive and "keep smiling!" If you smile, others will more likely smile with you.

People desiring to take a job as a facility and property manager often have no detailed plan on how to approach the job or some of the challenges which must be overcome in order to be successful. The chapters of this book present a roadmap that Frank Mitchell developed to gain knowledge of his department and build trust with his employees and his superiors. The primary character of the book is Frank Mitchell, whose name was selected because of the initials FM, which can also represent facility management. The book is divided into three parts covering the first week, the first six months, and the first year. At the end of each part is a list of questions that can be used for discussion and to develop and explore alternative solutions.

INTRODUCTION

Frank Mitchell sat in his office after a demanding and frustrating day, just like the many he experienced throughout his career. He was disillusioned because he needed additional funds, $250K, to replace an air handler that provided cooling for the research building. The Dean of Research kept calling Frank demanding something be done. Researchers were losing their experiments; most researchers were outraged. Frank's budget had already been reduced this fiscal year and he had no emergency fund.

Frank is a middle-aged administrator at the local university. He is confident, organized, and attentive to details. He approaches each day with a can-do attitude. His position, Director of Facility Management, is demanding. He thrives on the daily challenges, excitement, and mental stimulation provided by the job and the people with whom he works. Frank wants to help people and ensure building systems function as they should. His main focus is to support the university and its growing needs. He has come to the conclusion that the Operations and Maintenance (O&M) of buildings and grounds is his passion.

As he sat in his office, Frank ruminated about his life, the twists and turns and challenges of his journey, the mistakes he made, and how he stumbled into careers that he loved. Frank has been the Director of Facility Management at this university for 20 years. His prior career of 20 years had been in the military. After graduating from college, he accepted a commission as a second lieutenant in the Army Corps of Engineers. Frank never thought he would make the Army a career.

However, his decision to follow this path was rewarding. In addition to gaining valuable knowledge in engineering and managing facilities, Frank gained experience in working with, leading, and managing people from diverse cultures and education levels. In the Army, he commanded men and women at the platoon level, company level, and higher. He oversaw the operation of rock quarries, rock crushers, asphalt plants, and built and paved roads. He worked as the assistant resident engineer on a lock, dam, and powerhouse at a Corps of Engineers civil works project. He was the engineer project manager for the development, activation, and opening of the Army's National Training Center in the Mojave Desert.

Frank's last overseas assignment was as Director of Public Works at a military community in Europe. He thoroughly enjoyed this job because of the challenges and people with whom he worked. In his position, Frank oversaw the operations, maintenance, renovation of facilities, and new construction. He was responsible for nine million square feet of space and had over 900 employees. He also had 39 different nationalities to lead and manage, many of whom spoke languages other than English. Upon leaving the position, he was assigned to the Pentagon- a job and assignment he did not want and disliked very much. After twelve months in this new job, Frank decided to retire from the Army.

One Sunday, while he read the local newspaper, Frank spotted a job at a university for their Director of Facilities Management. He submitted his application and curriculum vitae. He was surprised when he received a call to come for an interview. After two months that included a half dozen interviews with various deans and vice presidents at the university, Frank was offered the job. He was ecstatic about the opportunity. After a discussion with his wife, Frank submitted his retirement paperwork with the Army. Two months later he was a civilian working at the university.

Frank's first day in his new job was interesting. He spent most of the day meeting people in other departments who would be his peers. In those days the facility management employees worked 7:30 A.M. to 4:00 P.M., Monday through Friday. He was sitting at his desk when at 5:25 P.M. the lights went out. Frank looked out the window and saw nothing but blackness—no lights. This was January when darkness came early. He knew this was not good. This was Frank's introduction to his new career.

PART ONE
FIRST WEEK PLAN

Chapter One
New Job

Point To Ponder: Checking cultivates confidence

Several weeks before beginning his new job and civilian career, Frank wondered what it would be like to work at a university. He contemplated what it would be like to not have a uniform to wear and instead select clothing for work each day. He was used to a daily regimen, camaraderie, and excitement. Now, being a civilian felt completely foreign. The university's relaxed environment and dress contrasted from his previous work experience. Had he made the right decision?

Frank spent time anticipating how his days would be spent. He knew from experience the importance of developing a plan to achieve specific goals. He decided to develop a plan of action that would provide him focus and direction. His experience solidified the need for detailed planning. He learned that prior to any military engagement or exercise, planning was critical. Details had to be considered, and rehearsals were essential. One of his favorite sayings—the maxim "check, check, and recheck"- would be prevalent throughout his plan. Frank knew that follow-up by checking cultivates confidence, efficiency, and effectiveness.

In the military, he knew that lack of good planning could impact the mission or, worse, get someone killed. Working at a university was not the same, but he thought that a lack of good planning could result in his loss of credibility, organization funding, and even employee staff. He considered planning to be extremely necessary if he were going to be successful.

Frank's plan of action would be a roadmap he could follow and adjust to help him navigate the job's complexities. Based on his previous experience—and knowing how he was when it came to working—Frank knew this civilian job would be taxing and demanding. But he also knew he was prepared. To build trust, Frank knew the importance of keeping his new boss, Steve Smith (Vice President of Design, Construction, and Facilities), updated on what he was doing in case there were questions from the university's leadership.

His prior training taught him:

1. Communication is critical to accomplish any mission,
2. Keeping superiors informed is a fine way to start building credibility, and
3. Cultivating trust is critical to developing strong work relationships.

Frank knew his roadmap had to be flexible and adaptable to any given situation. Having a roadmap as a guide seemed a good way to stay on track, learn, clarify the job, and eventually succeed. Frank decided to divide his roadmap into phases. His first phase would include the first week on the job. The second phase would consist of his first six months. The third phase would include following up on issues that surfaced during his first year. In each phase, he would summarize the issues he uncovered, explain what he learned, and decide on the next steps to take. This phased roadmap would also be used to keep his boss updated and set the stage for future actions.

In addition to the roadmap, Frank decided to **keep a daily journal**. He thought some of the entries may be short one-liners. In other cases, his journal entries might be longer due to the issue at hand. He thought the journal would be a good way to reduce stress, keep focused on achieving his goals, document information that could be lost over time, and increase his self-confidence.

Chapter Two
First Day

Point To Ponder: Shortcuts in FM can be dangerous

Frank awakened early because of the excitement of starting a new job. He planned to be at the university by 7:30 A.M. He showered, shaved, and decided to wear a sport coat, blue shirt, and tie, then leave the house at 6:30 A.M. He lived 30 miles from the university and was surprised at the traffic driving into the city. It took almost one hour to travel the 30 miles, arrive on campus, and find parking. He decided in the future he needed to leave home earlier.

The traffic bothered him, but it also provided him time to think and observe, an important tool in his line of work, and a necessity in morning traffic. Frank observed men shaving as they drove, women putting on makeup, and a car driving in the emergency breakdown lane in an attempt to pass other cars. He saw drivers with their heads down, perhaps reading messages or perhaps looking for information on their cell phones.

Frank thought about these drivers in comparison to facility employees. People can be careless and take shortcuts to accomplish tasks. When working with tools, electricity, or machinery, such action can be dangerous; sometimes it ends up more costly.

Frank glanced out the window while pondering this thought. Along the road were the flashing lights of a police car, the now-dented front end of the car that kept using the breakdown lane to pass cars illegally, and the clearly damaged car of the woman he had passed as she was applying makeup. Both drivers seemed engrossed in conversation with the police officer. Frank felt relieved neither car's occupant seemed hurt. He tucked away this anecdote as a good example of the necessity to think about your "time savers" at work and in life. Are they really beneficial?

Frank pulled into the university underground garage and parked. He stepped out of his car, took a deep breath, and put a smile on his face. He thought to himself, "Think positive. This is your first day and it will be great—a day you won't forget!"

That first morning, he reported to the Human Resources (HR) office. He was given a short general briefing on the university, received his identification card, and met Nancy Bright, the HR specialist who supported his department. Frank knew that Nancy would become important to him in the future; he wanted to begin establishing a positive rapport with her. Since he was not completely aware of university policies, he believed Nancy could help educate him on personnel policies and various personnel laws. Nancy suggested they meet later in the week.

On his way back to his office he stopped by his boss's office and introduced himself to the executive assistant to the Vice President of University Design, Construction, and Facilities. He knew this was another person with whom he had to develop a good rapport. Frank was astute at knowing how to play politics. Since his boss was involved in a meeting, he decided to walk back to his office.

Arriving at the office, he introduced himself to his administrative assistant, Rona King, and asked her to schedule a meeting after lunch with all the managers, foremen, and supervisors in the department. Rona had worked at the university for 20 years, but she had been in the Facility Management department for ten of those years. She seemed to be efficient. She was well-spoken and neatly dressed, but Frank would need time to determine her commitment and dependability. Frank thought to himself, "Time will tell."

He told Rona to let him know when everyone was gathered in the conference room. Getting to know the organization, individual sections, and people in the department was his primary focus. Information is key to good management. Knowing the number of employees who work in the department, their skills, work habits, and attitudes is also important.

Meanwhile Frank set up his office. He set up several facility management reference books from home on his shelves. He placed the table and four chairs in front of his desk so when he met with employees and visitors they could sit at the table. He did not like to meet from behind his desk because he thought it too formal; he didn't want people to think of him as a formal department head. His main focus was building trust and credibility with everyone with whom he met. Frank also mounted the whiteboard he purchased on the wall behind the table. He liked using the whiteboard when thinking and solving issues. At 1 P.M., Rona knocked on his office door to tell him that everyone was assembled in the conference room.

Walking into the conference room, he found it packed. There were 22 managers, foremen, and supervisors sitting around the conference room table and along the wall. As all eyes stared at him and the room became quiet, Frank thought, "You can hear a pin drop; don't say something stupid." Before he sat down, he walked around the room and shook everyone's hand, introducing himself.

As he looked each individual directly in the eyes, he thought, "I bet they're wondering what type of person I am and what changes I will make." It was important to look at each individual in the eyes to set the stage that he was now the leader of the department and this was his first step to build credibility and trust. He knew they wanted information about him—his background, education, and experience- to begin forming their opinions.

Frank opened the meeting by thanking them for coming and providing them with some of his background and experiences. When he finished, he asked each of them to do the same, focusing on what they did, the number of employees they supervised, where they worked (what buildings they supported), and how long they had been in the job. He took general notes, knowing that he would soon get to know each of them more intimately.

After the introductions, Frank asked for general information about the department, such as the number of employees, how the department was organized, how many buildings were maintained, how many square feet of building space were managed, how many acres of land were covered, and what technology was available and in use. One manager stated there were approximately 350 employees in the department. Another manager explained the department had three maintenance zones, each with 12–15 technicians; central shops consisting of plumbing, carpentry, lock and key, electrical (low voltage and high voltage), and HVAC (heating, ventilation, and air-conditioning); and landscape, grounds, custodial, garage, solid waste and recycling, small contracts, building automation controls, a stock room, and a work management center.

The custodial manager responded there were 61 buildings providing residential, administrative, athletic, and medical space for a total of 8 million square feet. The landscape manager mentioned there were 250 acres of land, which included athletic space, as well as 23 manicured garden areas which provided various parts of the campus with colorful flowering plants and flowers. The resource manager noted that technology was limited, adding that they had been trying for several years without success getting funding. Frank then asked for a copy of the department's strategic management plan, organizational charts, and job descriptions. Again, the resource manager explained they were very limited, but would get Frank what they have.

At the end of the meeting, Frank asked, "How often did you meet with the former director?" Several managers responded that the previous director had held various positions in the department for over 30 years and did not like to have meetings. After six months as Director, he decided to retire. Consequently, meetings were few and far between. Frank asked what the normal work hours were and was told 7:30 A.M. to 4:00 P.M. Monday through Friday.

Frank then decided that he wanted to schedule daily standing meetings. He thought they would provide a good way to learn what issues were surfacing and what actions were being taken, along with an opportunity to learn and understand his managers. So he decided to have daily meetings at 8:00 A.M. There were a few groans and comments made which Frank could not understand.

Frank explained, "Group meetings are important to get up to speed on issues and learn how the department operates. The meetings will be short, 15–20 minutes (max), covering a format of: what happened last night, what's happening today, and what's happening the rest of the week." Frank ended the meeting with a reminder: "We'll start tomorrow."

Later that day, after numerous "meet and greet" meetings, Frank sat at his desk. It was dark outside because this was January and darkness comes before 5:00 P.M. At 5:25 P.M., the lights in the building went out. Frank stood up and looked out his window. It was pitch black! Remembering that everyone left at 4:00 P.M., Frank wondered who was available. He called out for George Herman, his deputy director who was a mechanical engineer by training.

George had graduated from a technical university in the mid-Atlantic and his first job was as a mechanical engineer project manager in the university's

Design and Engineering department. After spending ten years in that department, a position opened in the Facility Management department for a deputy. George thought this would be an opportunity, so he applied and was selected. He had been in his position nearly one year when Frank was hired. George told Frank that he loved what he did and looked forward to gaining more experience in operations and maintenance.

George had an office down the hall from Frank. He responded, "I'm here." Frank, not having a flashlight, groped his way down the hall to George's office. Frank wondered where the emergency lights were. He asked George if there was someone who could take him around the campus. George responded that an HVAC technician who was on campus until 11 P.M. was the only person available.

Frank told George, "Call the tech on the radio and have him pick me up. There seems to be a widespread outage, and not only here on campus. Also, call the utility company." When the tech arrived, Frank jumped into the truck and introduced himself. He asked the tech if he knew where the emergency generators were located. When the tech responded, "I do," Frank indicated he wanted to see all of them.

About an hour later, they returned to the office and were greeted by George and Frank's boss. Asked for a status report, Frank explained that he had checked 35 emergency generators and that all were operating and providing emergency power to their buildings. George noted that the utility company had lost a generator at its plant across the river. That generator provided electrical power to the university's section of the city.

George added that the utility company was working at getting the backup online and expected to have power back within one hour. Approximately 45 minutes later, in fact, the power came back on. After asking George to remain on campus for another hour in case something came up, Frank decided to head home.

While driving home, Frank thought about his first day on the job and wondered how he would best learn the university buildings and grounds. He also made a mental note to check emergency lights in the office. He thought of this as he experienced the local frenzied, stop-and-go traffic, and the interruption of his normal fitness routine. By the time he arrived home, he had a plan.

He would leave home every morning at 4:00 A.M. This would allow him to beat the traffic and go to the local fitness center to get a one-hour workout, clean up, and get to his office by 6:30 A.M. Once he arrived he would walk parts of the campus and tour some of the academic buildings. He could then get back to his office by 7:30 A.M. and prepare for his 8:00 A.M. daily meeting.

Additionally, Frank planned to use this time to walk through various buildings, checking cleanliness and also checking mechanical rooms. He considered mechanical space as sacred because the equipment in these areas could be dangerous; they provided heating, cooling, ventilation, plumbing, and electrical systems that enabled occupants to accomplish their jobs in a safe, comfortable environment.

Frank felt strongly that mechanical rooms and electrical closets should always be locked, accessible only by authorized maintenance employees. He knew from experience that occupants and tenants often stored property (chairs, tables, desks, etc.) in these areas and in stairwells. From his perspective, that practice was a definite no-no because it was a fire code violation.

Chapter Three
First Week Meetings

Point To Ponder: Develop and share an operating and management philosophy

The first few days on the job Frank met with each manager and foreman in their respective offices and shops. It was important to meet in their spaces so that he could learn where each of them was located and get a feel for how they managed. He asked many questions.

While meeting with the carpenter shop foreman, he was surprised at a comment the foreman made, "We're all taking bets that you won't make it here a year." When Frank asked the foreman why he made that statement, the foreman replied, "We've had six directors in the last seven years."

Frank realized then the department was in chaos. No one knew what the directors' policies were. Each director implemented a set of policies and then left; the next director changed the previous policies and implemented a new way of operating. Managers and employees were in turmoil and confused. Again, Frank made a mental note to himself.

At one of the 8:00 A.M. daily meetings, Frank stated he wanted to review scheduled maintenance and repair projects on Friday of that week. He asked each manager to come to the meeting prepared to discuss the specifics of their projects. That Friday, the review of the projects began. Some of the managers and foremen brought their list of projects, but some did not. Frank was surprised at those managers and foremen who did not bring their project information, but he decided to conduct the meeting anyway with the information available.

He noticed there was no procedure established to identify work that needed to be done. He identified it as "seat of the pants" planning, which he was not used to. He decided he would get into more detail at another time.

After reviewing the projects, he dismissed everyone except those managers and foremen who did not bring their project list. In a firm statement, he told them that they should not underestimate him. He planned to be in the job for at least a few years. When he asked them to do something, they'd better do it, or suffer consequences. Before he dismissed them, he asked them if they were "crystal clear" on what he stated.

Following this meeting, Frank reviewed what had just taken place. He compared his experience to that of a new coach of a sports team: the coach doesn't know the players and the players don't know the coach. The players are apprehensive of the new coach and what changes will be implemented. The coach is distrustful of the players because he doesn't know their capabilities. For similar reasons, the coach may also be distrustful of the coaching staff.

Frank decided he would write an operating and management philosophy. His intent was to help his subordinate managers, foremen, and supervisors understand how he thinks and operates. He learned years ago the importance of knowing how to understand and manage your boss. Therefore, he wanted to help his subordinates learn how to manage him. Essentially, his operating and management philosophy would be a guide for them to be successful—to accomplish their personal needs and goals while concurrently developing a trustworthy and professional relationship with the director. He would take a team approach with the team working together to achieve goals.

Frank also thought describing his management philosophy would help cultivate his credibility and build trust with his subordinates. His philosophy consisted of two parts: first, overview and style, then, second, management philosophy. The overview and style section defined his thinking process. It explained that he is not a micromanager. He supports the concept of delegating authority and responsibility, and also likes to manage by walking around (MBWA) because he believes "knowledge is power." He is open-minded, welcoming both suggestions and productive critique.

The management and philosophy section covered his encouragement of awards and recognition, his open-door policy, and his pursuit of innovation to promote state-of-the-art technology. The section also included the need for communications, loyalty, counseling, fitness, training, property accountability, safety, and customer service. (See Appendix A for the example of Frank's style and philosophy.)

Concurrently, Frank wanted to know and understand his managers, foremen, and supervisors. He decided to make an effort to get to know each of their skills, strengths, weaknesses, personal goals, and expectations. He would do this by spending time with each of them, listening and observing.

Frank's administrative assistant, Rona, also scheduled meetings with the various deans, department chairs, and vice presidents of the many schools within the university. He met with them in their buildings and office areas. This provided him an opportunity to get to know their buildings, the building engineers who maintained their space, and the state of cleanliness, and to discuss issues that may be of immediate concern.

Frank also met with other department heads within the Design, Construction, and Facilities organization. The Director of Utilities gave him a tour of the central plant, which provided steam and chill water to 60 buildings. The Director of Design and Engineering provided an update on ongoing capital and major renovation projects. The Director of Administration updated him on personnel issues and the budget.

Frank focused much attention on his budget. The total annual budget was $15 million. It covered salaries, benefits, office expenses, utilities, rentals, maintenance and repair (grounds, building exteriors and roofs, interiors, electrical, heating, ventilation, and air-conditioning [HVAC], custodial, preventive maintenance, lock and key, carpentry, service contracts, moving, solid waste and recycling, and building alterations). He noticed there was no line item for training. He knew from experience that training must be continuous. As a minimum, training has to cover required safety tasks, emergency response, and technical subjects. This was an area on which he would concentrate in the future.

Late Thursday afternoon of his first week, Frank met with Nancy Bright, his department's HR specialist. Nancy had worked in HR for the last 15 years, since graduating from college. She was both intelligent and knowledgeable. Frank thought that despite any disagreements he might have with her, she seemed like someone in whom he could trust and confide. Nancy provided Frank information on university policies with which he should become familiar. Nancy also provided her perspective on various managers, foremen, and employees within the Facility Management department.

Before departing his office on Friday evening Frank decided to summarize what he had done during his first week. He wanted to summarize and inform his boss as to whom he met, what he learned, and potential issues he planned to review and examine. Frank thought this was a good way to keep his boss informed. It would also help him to keep a journal, which was important to Frank so that at the end of the year he could summarize what he had been working on. He then departed for home, knowing he would have at least an hour and a half in traffic to think about his first week on the job.

PART I DISCUSSION QUESTIONS

1. What is the advantage of having a roadmap when learning a new job?

2. How can a facility manager develop trust and credibility? Are they important?

3. As a manager new to an organization and the position, on which staff functions should you depend?

4. Do you think meetings with your subordinates, contractors, or service providers are valuable? Why? Why not?

5. Why should mechanical and electrical spaces always be locked?

PART TWO
THE FIRST SIX MONTHS

Chapter Four
Learning Everything

Point To Ponder: Identify strengths and weaknesses and look for opportunities and threats

Frank's first six months were busy. He spent 12–15 hours a day and sometimes weekends working to learn all he could about the facilities he was responsible to manage. He was driven and felt a responsibility to the people who used, occupied, and lived in the buildings. His wife even made comments that he spent more time working than he did with her and the family.

Because of his position he was invited every day to meetings with university leaders. He quickly learned that a university does not operate like the military. In the military, punctuality is a well-understood fact. The university does not operate the same. When a meeting is scheduled for 10:00 A.M., Frank would arrive at least 10 minutes early so he was ready. He learned that civilian meetings at a university never start on time; that was a major annoyance for him.

He spent most of each day visiting and attending other department meetings where he was asked questions about their facilities. Most of the time he did not have the answers and stated, "I will get back to you shortly." Of course, this meant he would have to track down the requisite manager to get an answer to the question. Once he had the answer, he then had to "close the loop" with the department head. He felt this was critical to develop his credibility. He also spent much time attending design review meetings, construction and renovation meetings, and staff meetings.

When it came to his department, he wanted to assess the facility management operations. He thought back to his days in graduate school where he learned the importance of using planning tools such as SWOT analysis (strengths, weaknesses, opportunities, and threats). This assessment would help him identify areas within the department that were performing well and other areas that require attention. He would begin this modified SWOT analysis by first identifying strengths and weaknesses and then, through later follow-up, look for opportunities and possible threats. Frank decided to start by learning how many employees were involved, their experience and knowledge, and any personnel issues.

He focused on:

- Grounds and landscape maintenance;
- Solid waste and recycling operations;
- Central shop operations (e.g., plumbing, electrical, HVAC, night operations, preventive maintenance, carpentry, lock and key, fire protection);
- Maintenance zone operations;
- Custodial cleaning;
- Service contracts (e.g., pest control, elevator maintenance, custodial cleaning, water treatment, fire protection);
- Garage (equipment, vehicle, and bus maintenance);
- Hazardous waste management;
- Energy management; and
- Emergency management.

Frank asked numerous questions. Among other areas, he specifically focused on the hours of work and night maintenance. He could not understand how a university, which operated 24/7/365 (because students lived on campus), had minimal night maintenance or emergency response capability. He also considered how, during the normal workday, preventive maintenance might be performed on major equipment- such as exercising water valves, cleaning fan coil unit coils, changing filters, and testing emergency generators under building load.

Frank also wanted to know and understand the department's vision, mission, and goals. When he asked to review them, he was told there were none. He made a note of this and planned to schedule a future discussion as to how they would be developed.

Chapter Five
Department Issues

Point To Ponder: Always plan for the worst case

In his third month (March) as director, the Vice President of HR told Frank the university would begin union negotiations starting in June. The maintenance employees were all members of the local union. Since the facility management department was the largest single department and had the most union employees in the university, Frank would be on the negotiating team.

The VP asked Frank to dig out his department strike plan and update it. When Frank responded, "What strike plan?" the VP replied, "If you don't have one, then you better start writing." Frank asked his subordinate managers if they knew of such a plan; they all claimed none existed. So Frank began searching for information on union strike plans.

He found very little existed. He decided on a two-step approach. He would draft something immediately as a stop-gap measure. Then he would have time to develop a more detailed follow-up plan because the union contracts ran for three years. For the immediate plan, he focused on all his non-union employees who had technical experience (plumbing, HVAC, and electrical). He assigned each of them responsibilities in the event a strike was implemented. He also contacted several non-union contractors who supported his department and asked if they would provide support if needed. The more detailed plan would take some time and research to develop, but at least he had a preliminary plan in place.

The day after the Vice President of HR contacted Frank, his boss emailed him that the university was planning to expand academic and research programs and various departments were going to have their budgets reduced. Because Frank's department had the second largest budget in the university, he was being asked to reduce it for the next fiscal year. In this specific instance, the reduction involved not filling all vacant positions. What Frank did not anticipate was the reductions would occur over each of the next few years, resulting in an overall reduction of the budget by thirty percent. He would ultimately get more involved with the reductions, their impact, and the process of managing the university facilities.

Frank delved deeply into the budget. He wanted to know how it was developed, who developed it, and what it covered. He asked many questions and learned that the budget was limited and lacked planning. He was used to having an organization strategic plan that covered three to five years into the future. His experience was that the strategic plan, which included the organization master plan and list of capital and other projects, fed into a mid-range plan, which looked 18–36 months out.

A large proportion of the mid-range plan usually fed the annual work plan. In Frank's mind, the annual work plan should start with each employee providing information on equipment, training, and potential project work to their manager. The managers would sift through the information and recommendations, hold internal meetings, and develop a list of O&M work and training as part of their recommended annual work. The lists for each shop, zone, and section would then be integrated at the department level. By participating in this process, the employees would feel they were each contributing to the advancement of the department's objectives.

The annual work plan would eventually solidify into the budget. Frank knew from his experience that at any given time, there were usually three budgets being prepared: the budget closeout, the current year budget, and development of the next fiscal year's budget. Frank wanted to explore these budgets in much greater detail, but for now, he was just trying to learn how budgets had been prepared.

Chapter Six
Manage by Walking Around

Point To Ponder: Patiently listen to all employees

Another important requirement that Frank established for himself was to get to know as many of the 350 employees by name as he could. Years earlier he had read a book that explained MBWA, management by walking around. The MBWA concept was developed in the 1970s at the Hewlett-Packard (HP) corporation. Authors Tom Peters and Robert Waterman coined the term "managing by walking around" in their 1982 book *In Search of Excellence.*

Essentially, the concept of MBWA explains that managers who get out of their offices and walk around meeting and speaking with employees are more successful; they help build trust and credibility in themselves. Frank liked the concept and incorporated this technique into the way he led and managed. He had success with this in the past.

His subordinates trusted him because he made an effort to listen to them and assist them any way he could. He would follow up on issues, then get back to each individual. MBWA was important for him because he wanted to learn as much as he could. He knew this would take some time, so lunchtime seemed a good way to begin. Frank also wanted to get a feel for all employees' knowledge, skills, and abilities (KSA). He understood that KSAs are the minimum competencies employees should meet regarding the specifications of their job descriptions.

Because his memory was not great, Frank knew that meeting with employees was going to be difficult. He would meet people and they would state their names, but he could often not recall because he focused too much on what to respond. Frank decided to make a concerted effort to focus on each individual when he met them. He developed a technique to help him. When someone stated their name, he would repeat it out loud first. Then he would focus on a characteristic of the individual that he could relate to that person.

He also read articles on improving listening skills. He concluded that listening was most important in cultivating relationships with people. So he practiced focusing his complete attention on what people were telling him. He recalled that years earlier, when he arrived home from a busy day, he would walk into the house and his wife would start telling him what went on that day. Frank would nod his head as she spoke, but at the same time was browsing through the mail or watching the news. As he thought about that, he felt disappointed in himself; he decided he had to listen at home as well as at work.

Frank used lunchtime to walk through buildings, looking for his employees who may be cleaning or performing some type of maintenance. As he approached the employees, he introduced himself by putting out his hand to shake theirs. The employees were surprised because no director had ever come to speak with them. He made an effort to always have a smile on his face. He knew from experience that people are more likely to gravitate toward individuals who smile, and they would be more apt to trust that person.

The primary employees with whom he spoke were custodians. These employees are always available in the buildings, sweeping, vacuuming, wiping, pulling trash, or dusting. When Frank introduced himself, he thought, "I think they are wondering 'why is he talking to me?'" From what Frank had determined by talking with various managers and supervisors, previous directors were too busy to walk around and speak with employees.

One afternoon later in the week, the custodial manager, Jeremy Brown, stopped by Frank's office and told him some of the comments being made by custodians. Jeremy had been in the custodial breakroom when they congregated for their lunch break. He heard them ask each other, "Did Mr. Mitchell visit with you?" Another custodian commented, "What a nice man. And what surprised me is he listened to me and wanted to know about me, how I was feeling, my family, and do I like what I do?"

Being a trustworthy leader was an important characteristic to Frank. When he said he would do something he always followed up. As an old cliché states, "his word was his bond." Frank wanted to cultivate a reputation of trustworthiness. He wanted to be known as a director who cared about his employees, one who was firm but fair.

Driving home Frank had another thought about all the employees. He decided to have birthday letters, condolence letters, and special occasion letters sent to employees. The next morning, he told Rona about his idea and put her in charge of developing the letters and adding key dates to the calendar to ensure they were mailed appropriately.

Chapter Seven
Policies and Procedures

Point To Ponder: Good management tools are important

The next area Frank delved into was the department policies and procedures. He asked his deputy George to provide a copy he could read over the weekend. This was an area that Frank wanted to fully and carefully understand. A facility management organization needs good management tools, such as policies and operating procedures, to navigate the myriad of issues that surface daily. These tools reinforce minimum standards and encourage positive behavior. In his previous experience he learned that facility management procedures fell into three categories.

These categories are:

1. normal day-to-day operating standard procedures,
2. more detailed maintenance procedures, and
3. procedures to follow during emergencies.

Frank knew that policies and procedures should be well-coordinated and provide the guidance on how to handle various issues on a consistent basis. George told Frank the department had only a few written policies and procedures. The department followed the university's policies and operated primarily by word of mouth. Frank emphasized to George the importance of having good policies and procedures.

He added they were going to start writing departmental policies and procedures immediately. Frank then directed his administrative assistant Rona to develop a standardized format for both policies and procedures. He told Rona to meet with Nancy, the HR specialist, to discuss the university's policies and how they relate to facility management.

Frank knew that policies are guidelines focused primarily on organizational activities that should or should not be performed. He shared examples with Rona of typical facility management policies that applied to employees, including time and attendance, appearance, professional conduct, health and safety, and training. He noted that these organization policies govern when employees come to work or call in sick, how they dress, safety when conducting their work, and training.

Procedures, on the other hand, focus on the process of getting something completed and are more narrative in nature than policies. For example, standard procedures, which are used daily, guide employees in how to process a work request. Maintenance procedures specify steps maintenance personnel should take to keep equipment operating properly and safely.

These procedures usually have drawings and photos, as well as checklists the technician should follow. Emergency procedures are similar to maintenance procedures but are not as detailed due to the situation at hand. Their purpose is to get the emergency under control as quickly as possible. Training is critical for all employees to understand each policy and the procedures applicable to them.

Once the format was established, Frank held a meeting with all the managers, supervisors, and foremen. He asked Rona to present the format. (See Appendix B for an example of Policies and Procedures.) Frank then directed each of them to keep notes on how tasks are accomplished, and any issues that arose. Frank asked Rona to schedule monthly meetings where they all could review the issues and notes, and then decide how best to proceed with a procedure.

Frank asked George to review each of the policy areas that arose in the meetings and coordinate with the specific university department that would be involved. For example, a time and attendance policy would be coordinated with human resources whereas a safety issue would be coordinated with either the risk management department or the safety and environmental department. Some policies and procedures would have to be coordinated with outside agencies such as the Occupational Safety and Health Administration (OSHA), the National Fire Protection Association (NFPA), and the American Society of Heating, Refrigerating, and Air Conditioning Engineers (ASHRAE).

Frank specifically asked about policies and procedures that focused on work management and preventive maintenance. Frank knew these were critical to manage resources wisely and for the overall effectiveness of operations and maintenance as it relates to quality customer service.

As university departments and individuals submitted work requests, their requests were received by a work management center, also called a call center or work reception center. Frank thought of the work management center as the heartbeat of facility management.

It was where work originated, then was coordinated and scheduled. He asked how the process worked, who decided where the work request was channeled, and how the request was tracked. He was told by the work management supervisor that approximately 40,000 work requests were processed annually. The information was entered into Excel spreadsheets. The work request was assigned to a custodial manager, shop foreman, or zone manager, who then assigned work orders to a technician. At the completion of the work order, a survey was sent to the individual who requested the work.

Preventive maintenance (PM) is at the heart of maintenance in any facility management organization. Frank understood this and queried Jim Askew, the asset manager who also oversaw the PM program. Jim explained that about 1,000 items had been identified as requiring PM, but the list had not been updated; therefore, some of the items had been replaced or removed. Although preventive maintenance work orders were issued to managers for scheduling, it was questionable as to whether they were being completed.

When he learned that PM tasks were scheduled during the normal workday, Frank asked how they could be completed when facilities were occupied, suggesting they may be better scheduled after normal work hours. Jim agreed but noted that the technicians' hours were during the regular 7:30 A.M. to 4:00 P.M. workday, Monday through Friday. In turn, Frank asked whether all the PMs were being completed, to which Jim responded they were not because of inconvenience to the employees using the space.

Frank pressed on, asking as an example how often fan coil units were cleaned and filters changed. Jim told him they were lucky if the coils get cleaned annually and the filters changed quarterly, adding it was a best-case situation. He explained further that some fan coil unit coils had not been cleaned for several years and filters were lucky to be changed annually. Frank was surprised; he then asked about indoor air quality issues. He thought to himself that this area needed to be studied and a solution found to enable all PMs to be completed as recommended in manufacturer operating and maintenance manuals.

Chapter Eight
Training

Point To Ponder: Training affects performance and reduces accidents

One of Frank's principal work objectives and sayings is "safety is number one." A safe workplace for employees, staff, faculty, students, and visitors is paramount. To achieve a safe building or campus there is a need for a good department training program for its technicians and managers.

Frank has always believed that training is essential. It ensures that the facility staff responds to any situation with self-confidence, knowledge, and understanding. From experience, Frank knew that by having equipment operate properly and following standardized procedures, training increases efficiency of equipment and cultivates employee ownership. His mantra is, "Informed and well-trained employees will contribute more to the organization by taking a personal interest and ensuring equipment operates safely and as it should."

As Frank thought about training, he recalled an incident that occurred a few years earlier involving a sprinkler system in a barracks. Soldiers were playing frisbee in the hallway. The frisbee clipped the sprinkler head, which then activated. The fire alarm alerted the public safety office, which then contacted the night maintenance technician.

When the technician arrived and saw the amount of water being discharged, he panicked. He stopped thinking clearly. The technician called Frank at home, at midnight, and explained the situation. Frank instructed the technician to calm down and think about where the shutoff valve would be located. When the technician replied that he didn't know, and expressed concern about there being so much water, Frank suggested he check the stairwell. Soon after, the technician reported to Frank that he found and shut the valve, but the water was still running.

Following Frank's prompts, the technician indicated he was on the third floor of five. Frank then led the technician to think about what he had just explained and to realize there remained two floors of water in the pipe above; therefore, the water would continue until it got to his level. Frank has a "share the wealth mentality" when it comes to information.

He wanted his managers and supervisors to have opportunities to attend regional and national conferences. This would enable them to learn what other organizations were doing with technology, planning, and other similar issues. Managers and supervisors could then bring that information back to the department, share it, and help implement it. Frank recognized that another positive impact of having a robust training program was that it would also help build the morale of employees, managers, and supervisors.

When Frank reviewed the budget, he could not understand why there was no line item for training. He asked how required training, such as backflow preventer maintenance and fire alarm maintenance, was funded. He was told that as training needs surfaced, funds from the Operations and Maintenance (O&M) account were used.

Of course, he understood the impact of doing this. Funds for O&M work are usually earmarked for specific noncapital projects and equipment replacement. Using those funds for training means the O&M project work doesn't get done. When that happens, the possibility of an emergency escalates because the department is now dependent on reactive maintenance.

Frank asked to see the training schedule. George and Rona indicated there was none. George explained that because of no budgetary funding, only minimal required training was provided. Frank then asked what the practice was with new hires- whether there was training orientation for new employees so they knew what acceptable practices were prior to taking on their new duties. He then continued, trying to learn how technicians were refreshed on new technologies, safety practices, and codes, and whether any cross-training of technicians was ever offered.

When Frank then inquired whether there was training on emergency responses for any building emergency that may occur, George indicated there was, but it was minimal. Frank looked at both George and Rona and said,

"We're going to change that!" Frank tasked Rona to start developing a department master training plan.

He told her the plan should define the specific training based on job descriptions, location of the training, time and date, who should participate, and who would be the instructor. This plan would also tie in with the operating procedures and policies, on which Rona was already working. The training had to be scheduled on the annual calendar so that employees (technicians) would know when specific training that affected them would take place. He added that for the first year the training wouldn't be perfect, but it would at least be a start. Next, Frank asked Rona to prepare a skills list to be covered by various types of training.

At a minimum, Frank wanted training to cover:

- basic first aid and CPR;
- confined space;
- lockout/tagout;
- basic fire protection systems;
- blood-borne pathogens;
- sexual harassment;
- workplace violence;
- understanding established protocols, policies, and procedures;
- emergency preparedness;
- shelter in place;
- weather emergencies;
- overview of safety codes and regulations;
- slips and fall protection;
- hazardous materials;
- indoor air quality;
- how to be observant of safety and maintenance issues; and
- National Incident Management System.

Concurrent with Rona developing the training plan, Frank asked her to estimate the cost of an annual training program based on the plan. Cost should include hours of training per individual. Frank also expressed his thoughts that training should include tips for all employees to be vigilant and observant, as an extra set of eyes and ears, for any criminal or terrorist type activity. Additionally, as employees walked through their buildings, their observations and informal inspections should include safety and hazardous conditions, maintenance issues requiring attention, physical security issues, building cleanliness issues, waste management sanitation, landscape and grounds issues, facility employee appearance, and customer service.

Frank directed Rona to also ask the managers for their input and employee assessment. Managers need to know their employees' strengths and weaknesses. Additionally, he asked her to work with the managers to develop a list of metrics which could be used to measure the success of the training and to identify areas that needed more emphasis. Frank explained to Rona that once they understand the need and had the beginning of a list, they could assign the various employees to the training, showing the hours needed for each employee. From that, they could then develop a schedule for training and the cost for the rest of the year.

For this first year, Frank planned to take the funds from planned projects. He didn't like doing that, but he had no choice. However, in the following year's budget, he would include a line for training because he knew that training would be the best investment of time and money. He also planned to brief his boss and other university leaders who make financial decisions about the importance of training and the potential negative impact of not funding a robust training program.

For training resources, at least initially, Frank directed Rona to check with the various vendors, companies, and associations with which the department has an affiliation, adding that most of them would not charge for the training. As examples, he listed companies that provided cleaning supplies, maintenance supplies and materials, HVAC water treatment, and engineering firms that are doing capital projects on campus. Some of these organizations would also provide "lunch and learns." Frank also suggested Rona check with Nancy in HR because human resources departments sometimes provide leadership development courses for managers and supervisors. He further noted that with current technology, there may be training available through YouTube and other media.

Frank continued thinking about training when driving home. He wondered what the turnover (churn) rate of the department was, and also the average age of employees. When Frank arrived home, he texted Nancy and asked about those two questions; Nancy responded that she would check in the morning.

The next morning Nancy texted Frank that the churn rate was relatively low, 10–15%, because employees liked working at the university and the benefits. For the second question, she stated the average age of employees was 57 years. Frank was gratified to read that employees enjoyed working at the university, but he was concerned about the average age because the older employees would be thinking of retiring. That thought caused Frank to think about the legacy knowledge of employees when they left the university. He considered how to plan for tomorrow today by capturing the information senior employees have in their heads, especially before they leave.

Frank reflected on an emergency that he experienced earlier due to a lack of information. A water pipe had burst on the third floor of a building Frank's department maintained. The plumbing foreman knew the details of the building in his head, but he was on vacation. No one else in the shop knew the location of the water shutoff. Consequently, 10 gallons of water per minute flooded the lower levels of the building. It took two hours to locate the "as-built" drawings and determine the location of the shutoff valve. As a result, the flooded building sustained several hundred thousand dollars in damage. Had the valve shutoff information been readily available, the building disaster and thousands of dollars in repairs could have been averted.

Frank decided to meet with Nancy and George to discuss a process for collecting legacy information from retiring senior managers. Several weeks before their actual retirement Frank made it clear he wanted the retiring manager to spend time with the archivist and update the paper "as-built" drawings. They all agreed this was a good start. The archivist would eventually have the plans and other documents digitized so they could be pulled up on cell phones or other devices. They all knew this would take time to accomplish, but it would lead to decreasing reliance on employee recollection of building plans.

Frank thought technology, including artificial intelligence, could help, especially in emergencies. Once implemented, technology could be added to the training plan. Technicians and managers could be taught to pull up information about buildings, systems within buildings, and emergency plans. This aspect of technology and training would save time of going to the archives to locate operations and maintenance manuals or as-built plans. Frank thought such training would not only save time, but ultimately money, which could have a positive impact on the budget. All he had to do was determine how to proceed.

Chapter Nine
Culture and Perception

Point To Ponder: Organization culture is learned therefore it can be altered

Frank met with George and summarized his thoughts based on his few months of gathering information about the department. Frank stated his perception that the culture of the FM employees was they do their basic job functions as depicted in their job descriptions. Maintenance was often performed in a reactive manner because of other funding priorities. Although there was a preventive maintenance program for buildings, facility equipment, and vehicles, it was very limited, and occasionally it was not accomplished. Employees had minimal tools, and parts were challenging to obtain in a timely manner. Hence, there was no sense of urgency.

George suggested the employee perception was they were protected by human resources and the union. Consequently, the director had personnel challenges when he tried to make changes. Meanwhile, customer and stakeholder perception was that work was not done in a timely way. Customers had to call in requests for work to be done. Work was then assigned to shops and zones using Excel spreadsheets, and not a computer maintenance management system (CMMS).

Frank was astounded—in the 21st century and at a growing university— that Excel spreadsheets were used for tracking work. He added that change was needed quickly. Frank further noted that, when work was completed, the customer was asked to sign off. Yet follow-up by trade personnel was neither automatic nor consistent. Hence, quality management was non-existent.

Frank realized that to change the organization culture, he had to understand it first. He also knew that to change minds, open hearts, and build trust, leaders must understand the people and the culture, including their customs and beliefs. Frank decided to meet with all his managers to discuss the organization's culture. He also invited Nancy, the HR specialist, to assist. Before the meeting, Frank asked Nancy to gather the facility management department's diversity statistics.

At the meeting Nancy presented the cultural statistics, summarizing the diversity breakout within the department: 52% White, 20% Black, 19% Hispanic, 5% Asian, and 4% other (various nationalities). At that point, Frank explained that culture is defined by national background, race/ethnicity, socioeconomic class, gender, and age. He continued that each of these play a role in shared beliefs, values, and norms, all of which affect people's behavior. George then asked how the managers could understand the employees and change the organizational culture. Nancy responded, "Culture is learned. It's the norm as to how and where an individual was raised."

Frank then asked everyone what this means from a practical standpoint. He noted that because culture is learned, it can be changed. He next focused on the point that the goal was not to change the individual culture, but the organizational culture. He added that because organizational culture is learned, it can be unlearned.

When the central shops manager asked what that ultimately meant, Frank spoke about changing the habits of the employees. Frank expanded his response, noting that individual habits can be changed by focusing on a shared set of values and rules about what is important to the organization. Furthermore, he added, habits can be changed by focusing on those specific values that contribute to the achievement of the FM department's mission and vision.

According to Frank, these values should be reflected in the department's efforts to support the university staff, faculty, students, visitors, vendors, contractors, government agencies, and the department's own employees. He used this point to renew his call for good departmental policies and procedures, and a vision, mission statement, and department goals. These efforts would influence the way the department's employees talked, dressed, and responded to customers, and the way they accomplished their work tasks. Thorough, careful, and thoughtful execution would lead to a change in old habits. Following

Frank, Nancy told the group of managers "this is not going to be easy ... and it's going to take time and consistent effort. I'm here to help all of you where I can."

By this time all the managers were listening and thinking about what had been said. Frank looked at each manager and wondered how many of them were taking this discussion seriously.

When George asked where the processes started, Frank responded with three key steps:

- Start by being flexible when communicating—meaning face to face, using social media, and not being judgmental.
- Practice listening skills to focus on issues that the employees cope with at work and at home. Be curious when listening.
- Show employees respect for themselves, their knowledge, and their experience.

Frank added that these steps would not be easy and would require consistency and firmness. After a moment's reflection, Frank commented about uniforms provided to the employees. He observed that some employees don't wear their uniform, preferring dungarees with shabby shirts and jackets. Frank suggested that one specific area to focus attention was professionalism, including that employees wear their uniforms.

He added that all the uniforms are made of synthetic fabric, which was fine for some trades, but that electricians, and perhaps even HVAC technicians, should wear cotton uniforms. When George asked why cotton, Frank explained that in case of fire, which these technicians are more prone to, cotton will burn whereas synthetic fabric will melt onto the skin and be more difficult to remove. Frank then asked George to meet with the uniform vendor and explain the desired change.

Frank summarized the nearly two-hour meeting, noting that change in organizational culture was doable, but would take time and continuous effort. It would require everyone to change their habits and learn more about the employees. He ended the meeting by sharing an experience from his military days.

He told the group, "When you and your soldiers are in combat, you want to trust the soldiers you're with because the lives of all of you depend on trust for each other; that's one reason the group is known as the 'band of brothers.' This is the reason squad leaders know specific information about all their soldiers: their complete names, where they are from, their family (including kids' names), problems they may have, and so forth." Frank said the meeting had been long but beneficial, and he would have Rona schedule a follow-up soon.

Chapter Ten
Asset Management and Preventive Maintenance

Point To Ponder: Asset Management database is critical for strategic planning

Frank kept thinking about an overall strategic plan for the department. But before he could start developing such a plan, he needed to know what the assets were and their condition. He wanted to review the physical asset inventory and review the long-term capital replacement plan. Frank knew that buildings change; equipment becomes obsolete or breaks down and eventually has to be replaced. He asked Jim Askew (the asset manager) to see the asset register and inventory.

Frank expected a register that contained information on maintenance and operations schedules, O&M cost for each asset, cost of utilities for each facility, and information on leased facilities. However, Jim responded that, when he took over his current position, there was no inventory. He has been trying to develop one himself. Frank was frustrated, knowing that without a good asset management database, he could not implement an effective facility strategic plan that would include an operations and maintenance plan. Nor could he develop a good preventive maintenance program. They had no idea what the asset life cycle of the equipment was because they didn't have a database. As a result, there was no asset replacement/renewal plan.

Jim Askew has been with the university for five years. His background was HVAC. He came to the university from a private company where he managed a small team of trade technicians. From discussions with Jim over the previous two months, Frank considered Jim dedicated to doing the best he could as asset manager; he wanted preventive maintenance to succeed. It appeared to Frank that Jim was not being supported. He was trying to add information and update his asset spreadsheets and was doing it whenever he could find the time. Unfortunately, he had very little support for updating the asset database.

Preventive maintenance (PM) is planned maintenance. It involves scheduling periodic condition inspection, lubrication of moving parts, adjusting and possible recalibration, cleaning, repairs, and replacement of parts and equipment. Frank knew PM is a relatively inexpensive and effective process. It minimizes unscheduled repairs and downtime by providing for a systematic, periodic servicing of equipment as well as cleaning of buildings and equipment.

Planning and scheduling preventive maintenance activity means the right maintenance will be provided at the right time at the lowest possible cost. The intent of PM is to avoid reactive and unplanned maintenance, which is work that was unscheduled and unbudgeted. A good PM program can reduce the organization's exposure to potential expensive breakdowns and associated emergencies; it also lessens their impact on customers.

Frank knew that there would always be unplanned maintenance. His years of experience indicated the ratio of planned maintenance should hover around 80 percent, with unplanned maintenance at 20 percent. However, George and Jim told Frank the ratio for the department was the reverse, probably 20 percent planned and 80 percent unplanned. The three men looked at each other and realized they had a challenge ahead of them.

Frank explained to George and Jim that his years of involvement demonstrated that an effective preventive maintenance program should be one that meets the following criteria:

- Prevent unexpected failures,
- Maximize vehicle and equipment availability,
- Furnish safe equipment to the users,
- Reduce downtime and repair costs,
- Extend useful life of the equipment, and
- Increase reliability.

From his experience, Frank knew that sizable cost savings will result from a well-defined and implemented preventive maintenance program, including from the prevention of breakdowns. He knew that in performing preventive maintenance, it is necessary to replace parts and sometimes equipment—a significant expense. However, this additional expense is offset by a reduction in the additional costs associated with downtime. Any decrease in work interruptions and delays also leads to better use of personnel resources, further reducing the overall cost of the operation. Frank also knew that reducing the impact on customers from breakdowns and downtime has a positive impact on the department's reputation as it relates to quality management and customer service.

As an aside, Frank stopped for a moment and thought of an incident which occurred years earlier relating to PM. One of his buildings contained a Specially Compartmented Information Facility (SCIF) for highly classified material and computer systems. This facility had to remain operational at all times. The 600KW emergency generator supporting this facility was tested monthly. However, it was only tested under building load annually.

One day, during a storm, the local power grid went down. The generator did not energize. After investigating Frank learned the problem was the transfer switch failed to automatically transfer the load to the emergency system. The transfer switch had not been PM'd. Frank learned a valuable lesson that almost cost him his job. He made the point to Jim to include testing transfer switches with emergency generators. If the building load cannot be transferred to the generator then get a load bank to simulate the building load.

After brief talks with George and Jim, Frank deduced that implementation of an effective asset management plan and PM program would require a culture change at all levels. The technicians had to be trained to catch all defects when performing preventive maintenance, something they were not currently being forced to do. The building, equipment, and facility users needed to diligently bring their issues to the attention of the FM department; that seldom happened. For the success of an effective asset management plan and PM program, management needed to encourage and enforce the established policies and procedures. However, these policies and procedures were essentially nonexistent. Thus, there was little emphasis.

Jim did find the existence of preventive maintenance sheets for a preventive maintenance program. The intent to advance a preventive maintenance program existed, but, in reality, there was very little preventive maintenance for facilities, equipment, grounds, or vehicles being conducted. Most of the work was performed on a corrective (reactive) maintenance basis when requested by the various departments.

There were no PM kits available in the stockroom. PM kits are needed to support the PM program. When the preventive maintenance for a building or equipment is scheduled, the concerned shop should have a list by make and model of the equipment that will require servicing. Suppose an air handler at a building site requires servicing. The shop should have the asset parts kits ordered in advance so the kit is available and ready to pick up prior to servicing the equipment. This planning results in considerable savings of time and resources while reducing downtime for the customer.

Jim reasoned that one reason for the lack of a good preventive maintenance program was the lack of availability of the parts and resources needed to effectuate a timely program. Furthermore, the stockroom did not have the adequate parts because there was no asset management plan. There was very little automation in the shop management area for work order control or inventory control. The lack of asset management information made it more difficult for the shops to order parts kits and for the stockroom to have the kits readily available.

Frank realized that facility management currently did not have an up-to-date asset inventory of critical equipment for each building. A comprehensive inventory- including make, model, and serial number of each piece of equipment- was needed. It would assist in ordering parts, scheduling PM, and reducing downtime. As an example, the department needed to know the type of AC unit in each building, the make and model of the generator, and the lighting system.

The shops did not have an automated mechanism for scheduling preventive maintenance. Instead, the shops scheduled work on an ad hoc basis. This procedure resulted in too many peaks and valleys in their workload requirements. The shops had no idea of the quantity of workload they might have on a given day. Frank could tell that Jim was frustrated that there was no asset management plan and no effective annual preventive maintenance in place.

Jim indicated he could not find labeling or numbering of equipment in the university. Labeling or numbering spare parts, vehicles, generators, water pumps, or any other asset would help the university to methodically track, sort, search, and assist when the FM department was ready for computerization. Frank knew the preventive maintenance program should be refined and expanded to include buildings, safety equipment, grounds, and vehicles. The concept of PM kits for ordering parts and supplies should be adopted to reduce downtime and improve equipment availability.

All facility assets should be labeled to include buildings, vehicles, spare parts, and other critical assets that would assist when the department was ready for automation. Jim thought that part-time student workers could accomplish this task. Barcoding would be advantageous to use since it would save time and be cost effective. An optical scanner could scan the code and send that information to a computer in order for the technician to access the equipment data file.

The success of the asset management plan and PM program could be enhanced by a commitment from top officials. Frank decided to write a memo to all departments, outlining the critical need of asset management and preventive maintenance and asking for their support in helping the FM department personnel achieve these requirements. George, working with Jim, began preparing a list of equipment and key components by building to reduce downtime when ordering parts, servicing, and scheduling preventive maintenance.

The list would be the start of establishing PM kits. They agreed to use part-time engineering students to help prepare the list. Frank then briefed his boss on what they were planning to do. He wanted him to understand this effort was going to take time and money.

Chapter Eleven
Automation

Point To Ponder: Comprehensive technology equates to efficient data and building management

Frank was reflecting back to an earlier discussion about not having a computer maintenance management system (CMMS), no effective asset management or PM program and using Excel spreadsheets for work orders and asset data. He was really concerned. He thought these were major deficiencies, especially during a time of exploding new technology.

Relying on Excel spreadsheets to process work orders was not the same as having a centralized database that included and integrated all FM assets. In addition, working with spreadsheets meant employees had to rely on their experience and memory. Having a database to pull up asset information and coordinate all aspects of O&M minimizes the legacy issues that too often occur when a veteran employee departs and a new one arrives.

Frank knew the university was expanding and adding new research and academic programs. This growth would lead to requirements for more space, more and newer types of building equipment, and additional staff, faculty, and students. There was no way his department could support these changes without a modern CMMS. In addition, the CMMS would help minimize detrimental impacts to the buildings and help avoid unplanned and expensive repairs.

A CMMS would ensure that all necessary data was available for evaluation, tracking, and reporting. Frank knew that a facility department aspiring for superb quality management and customer service depended on daily inspections of facilities, a good PM program, and a thorough, complete asset database. Deficiencies identified should be captured and entered into the CMMS as work orders, so they could be tracked and corrected. Also, Frank thought about the preventive maintenance program. PM schedules should be initiated by the department asset manager; any deficiencies, costs, or equipment changes should be included in the CMMS database.

The database could store information on each piece of equipment or asset. It would eventually cover tens of thousands of pieces of equipment, essentially acting as a cross-linked filing system. The database would include various types of files in categories such as: equipment, preventive maintenance, work order, work history, labor, schedule, inventory, inventory transaction, vendor, parts requisition, purchase order, and history. The CMMS would help quantify problems by cost center, equipment and machine, floor, and building, accounting for all labor, materials, and outside costs. In the long run, a CMMS would save time and money.

Frank needed someone who could lead this effort and follow it through. He knew this endeavor would be difficult, taking many months or even years to make a decision on a system, determine the cost, get authorization to proceed with purchase, determine which modules were essential and affordable, and finally implement the system. Frank thought Bill Heard, his resource manager who had been in place for three years, might be the manager to lead the effort. Bill knew the organization, was respected by everyone, and understood the budget and the obstacles for funding that would be encountered. Bill also had an innate ability with technology.

Frank met privately with Bill and asked if he would lead this project. Bill was ecstatic; no one previously would consider him for this type of endeavor. Frank told Bill that they were going to have a standing meeting every week to develop their strategy for the department plan to acquire a CMMS. In their first meeting, Frank explained that, as a minimum, the system should have the following modules: work order system, asset management database capability, and equipment and inventory management.

Later, they might also want to expand into an Integrated Work Management System (IWMS) involving emergency preparedness, project management, fleet management, sustainability, etc. Frank emphasized that whatever platform was selected should be one that could be expanded to meet the department's growing needs. It should also be a platform that could easily provide instant access to facility intelligence. Bill was not familiar with the term *facility intelligence*. Frank explained it covered everything they would need to know about the facilities, especially for emergencies.

Frank told Bill about a catastrophic experience, years earlier, which occurred the day after Christmas. A chill-water (CHW) line broke behind a barracks. The maintenance person called Frank at home and in a very agitated way explained there was a huge hole behind the building caused by a water leak. Frank thought ok and, in a nonchalant way, asked how big. The maintenance person explained-- BIG, as big as a tractor-trailer.

Frank thought to himself, maybe I should go check this. He drove in. The maintenance person met him on the main road, and they walked to the location. Sure enough, the hole was huge. Frank's first thought was to shut off the water, but where is the shutoff valve? Frank called his plumbing foremen to come in. Together they checked the archives and found the CHW pipe plans. Then they went to search for the shutoff valve. They eventually found it buried under garden mulch. It took almost three hours.

Once the CHW was shut off Frank stood looking at the hole and wondered where the soil had gone. The three of them then went into the building and Frank wanted to check the mechanical room. When they opened the door, they found the soil, now mud, four feet deep. The mud flowed down the building areaway and into the mechanical room, covering and coating all of the equipment. The areaway allows direct access to the basement mechanical room enabling equipment to be easily removed or added.

Frank thought how are we going to get this cleaned up? He decided to call in all his maintenance employees, issued them shovels, and they began moving and pushing the mud to the areaway. He next called for a city pumper truck and placed it at the top of the areaway with its long snout sucking up the mud. It took almost a week to suck out the mud and dispose of it. Once the mud was removed all the equipment: air handlers, boilers, pumps, hot water heaters and tanks, valves, etc. had to be cleaned before the systems could be activated and the building reoccupied. This was tedious work and required much patience.

Thankfully, it was a holiday period and the building was minimally occupied. Employees worked 12-hour shifts in order to have the building ready when the holiday period ended and occupants returned. If we would have had facility intelligence of the CHW piping and building plans immediately available on a laptop or iPad we could have minimized the damage and cost. This experience taught me a valuable lesson I will never forget.

Getting back to the CMMS issue Frank knew that this effort to obtain a CMMS, and eventually an IWMS, would take significant funding and perhaps years to get implemented. His first directive to Bill was to develop estimates on what this effort would cost, then assemble a PowerPoint set of slides. After rehearsing their presentation, he and Bill would brief the leadership and make their case.

Frank also instructed Bill to include the most pressing maintenance needs, the cost of the system, and the cost of training. He gave the option of phasing in some of these programs. He also recommended that Bill determine what hardware was currently available within the department for employees: computers, iPads, laptops, etc.

Next, Frank suggested that Bill work with Jim Askew, who was overseeing the asset management program along with preventive maintenance. He noted that Jim might have some ideas that should be considered. George, Bill, and Jim, as well as other managers, had great ideas, job experience, and motivation. Frank was thankful for their work and support.

Frank also had questions about the Building Automation System (BAS). He asked the central shops manager, Paul Larson, how old the system was, how many buildings had the automation, and what changes Paul thought should be made. Paul had been the manager of central shops for five years. His background and experience were in HVAC. He told Frank the BAS system was relatively old, had been installed 30 years ago, and controlled the HVAC and energy system in 30 buildings. Paul indicated the system needed to be upgraded and expanded.

Frank indicated to Bill, Jim, and Paul that he wanted the three of them to collaborate and determine immediate system upgrades and future expansion to include lighting, elevators, and fire protection; how much the total efforts would cost; and how long it would take to implement the plan. Also, because of environmental concerns, Frank wanted them to draft a policy summarizing the ASHRAE 62.1 requirement for using outside air. He recommended they meet weekly to discuss all of these issues.

At the next morning's 8:00 A.M. meeting, Frank explained that one of his ultimate goals was to outfit each department manager, foreman, and technician with an iPad or laptop wherein building information on work orders, materials ordered, work orders closed, and information readily available for first responders could be pulled up while in the field. Technology was of critical importance to the future of the department. This technology upgrade would also provide a way for the department to help solve future legacy information issues when senior employees retired. Frank told Rona and George that technology would have to be included in the department's policies, procedures, and training.

Chapter Twelve
Procurement and Contracting

Point To Ponder: Procurement and contracting involves operations, maintenance, repair, supplies, and services

The procurement process was another area Frank wanted to understand in much detail. Everything the department did required procurement of operations, maintenance, repair, supplies, and services. Bob Brown, the manager of the materials control (stock room) section, told Frank they ordered maintenance supplies and vehicle repair parts, coordinated with vendors, and ordered emergency support equipment such as electric heaters, fans, sandbags, and coolers. The section also tracked all purchases.

Bob had been at the university for 12 years. He had first worked as a clerk in the IT department's stockroom. When the manager position opened in the FM department, Bob applied and was selected. He had an associate degree in business and seemed well suited for this position. Bob was interesting to speak with and came across as knowing what he was doing to support the department.

Frank also met with Ed Fingle, Director of Contracts, and asked what contract services the department managed. He was surprised at the list: elevator maintenance, pest control, solid waste disposal, fire extinguisher certification, fire protection service (including fire pumps and quarterly testing and inspection of dry-pipe sprinklers), automatic door servicing, independent elevator inspection service, HVAC system cooling tower water treatment, glass repair, storm water sand filter cleaning, sanitary sewer jetting, grease trap cleaning, fire hydrant flow testing, and annual cleaning of diesel fuel tanks (especially those supporting emergency generators). Frank wanted to know how much was spent on service contracts annually, but that number was not immediately available. Frank guessed it was probably around $1 million, maybe a little more.

Ed told Frank that they followed the university's procurement policies and procedures for goods and services. Goods were purchased using purchase orders (POs) for one-time purchases and blanket purchase orders (BPOs) for goods purchased over a period of time. Frank knew from his experience that a purchase order was a written contract between the department and a vendor or contractor using a standard form. A one-time PO was good only for the one time it was used. By contrast, a blanket purchase order was for a specific timeframe, for example one year.

At the end of that time, the BPO would be reviewed and modified as required. Also, both POs and BPOs had monetary limits. In Frank's previous positions, he had signature authority up to $50,000. At the university, his signature authority was limited to $5,000. His subordinate managers each had a limit of $1,000. Ed further explained that service contracts were bid based on the developed scope of work (SOW). (A SOW explains the specific tasks to be accomplished, whereas a service-level agreement defines the standards and expectations.)

Frank asked Bob what the protocol was in emergency situations when specific materials or equipment were needed quickly, and maybe additional personnel. Bob responded that the procedures had some wiggle room for unusual one-time actions, like during an emergency. Frank remembered, and shared with them, that he had done something similar years earlier when he needed additional employees for snow removal. In that case, he had included in the custodial contract that the contractor would provide people to support emergency situations, as long as they were given 24-hours' notice. He found the advantage of this partnering contract was the employees were known and had already been vetted by the contractor.

Frank then asked about the service contracts. He knew his department could not directly provide all the services. Many of the services were specialized and required specialty service contractors, for example, fire protection and window washing. Frank was curious how service contractors were selected. Ed responded that they developed service-level specifications, which were the minimum level of services acceptable to meet the requirements; the specifications defined the standards.

Next, Frank asked Bob if they had ever used a service-level agreement with a vendor for Just-In-Time (JIT) delivery, for example, for HVAC filters. When Bob asked why, Frank explained that Just-in-Time delivery was developed in the 1950s for Toyota. This concept requires vendors to consolidate supplies and deliver them when needed.

Frank explained that changing a building's worth of filters was a big job, took considerable time, and required much storage space for the filters. If they had a service contract with a vendor and a service-level agreement to deliver filters for a building within 24 hours, then the vendor would obtain and store the filters until they were needed. That would save storage space, which is usually a building loading dock. However, the supply chain could be impacted.

As a result, they needed to know the critical parts and materials requirements and always keep a basic load of them in stock to be available in an emergency or if the supplier could not deliver due to supply disruption. Frank emphasized that this requirement should be part of the emergency plan. He then recommended that Bob, Ed, Paul, Jim, and George collaborate to develop the basic list of critical, high-demand parts and materials to be included as part of the emergency plan. Once the list was assembled, they should purchase the materials and parts, find a place to store them, and develop a plan to rotate so this "basic load" was always available, even during a logistics disruption.

Continuing on, Frank told Ed he had heard rumblings about the elevator service contractor. The contract was due to end in 90 days and contract requests for proposals (RFP) had been sent to various elevator contractors. Frank was concerned about this service contract. He wanted seamless implementation, no disruptions, and a smooth transition to a new contract. The university had 200 elevators and two escalators. Vertical transportation was a serious issue; especially with more faculty, staff, and students having disabilities and using wheelchairs.

Frank asked to see the proposed contract, which he intended to read over the weekend. Since this was such an important contract, he also asked about the plan for making the transition from the outgoing to the incoming contractor. He knew this plan had to be communicated to all customers and clients; it could have a negative impact on the reputation of the department if not handled seamlessly.

Frank recalled a similar concern in a previous job. The selected contractor had the optimum bid but subsequently stated there was $90,000 worth of deficiencies left by the outgoing contractor that had to be corrected. Frank responded that they didn't have that amount available in our budget; he would have to get back to them. He then met with the legal, finance, and contracts offices to seek recommendations. The next week Frank met with the new elevator contract president, stating that the contractor would have to absorb that cost.

The president responded that he could not do that because it was not in his original bid. From his meetings and his own reading of the contract, Frank was prepared. He countered to the president of the elevator company. "You take on the $90,000 cost, and we'll give you a ten-year contract." The elevator contractor president thought for a minute—it was dead quiet in the room—and responded, "You have a deal."

Frank told the story as a means of letting his team know he had experience negotiating contracts; it was important to think outside the box and consider contract incentives. He wanted them to know there's always a way for both sides to win during contract negotiation. Partnering with contractors and vendors can be a benefit to FM departments, if done correctly with the right contractor and vendor. Just keep it legal!

Chapter Thirteen
Emergency Management Plan

Point To Ponder: Command, control, and communication prior to, during, and after the emergency is essential

Frank asked his deputy George to see the department's emergency management plan. He wanted to read about how the department managed snow and ice. He also wanted to review how the plan applied to storms, natural disasters, infectious disease, and emergencies. It was still winter and there had not been any significant snowfall since December.

Frank was concerned about a major snowstorm which the National Weather Service indicated could materialize within the next week. George said the department did not have a dedicated facility management emergency plan. The university's emergency management plan was the plan they used.

George explained that, for snow emergencies, the department brought in people as needed. The landscape and grounds employees were the ones who came in to plow, clear sidewalks, building entrances, and stairs. Frank asked about the other trade employees, custodians, and administrative staff. George stated they never came in.

Frank wondered why everyone in the department was not considered "essential" and required to come to work during a major snow event, or for any emergency. Frank added this issue too to his growing list of areas to examine in more detail. However, because of his experience on his first day on the job (loss of electrical power), he planned to write something over the weekend on command, control, and communications during an emergency. He knew that in an emergency people would look to him for advice and direction. He had a responsibility to keep people safe and property protected. Along with that responsibility came accountability, both of which he took seriously.

On Monday morning, he and George discussed further what he had developed over the weekend. He told George that, if an emergency occurred, the work management center (WMC) would become the central focus of information collection. He directed George to immediately train everyone in the WMC on what to do and whom to contact if an emergency occurred. During an emergency, the WMC would be known as the Facility Emergency Operations Center (FEOC) and would provide information to the overall University Emergency Command Center.

Before any information was passed upward, it had to be cleared by the facility management duty officer—in this case Frank, since the other managers had not yet been trained. Frank knew from experience that, if information is sent forward before it has been verified, there was a possibility of confusion and chaos if that information subsequently changed.

Frank also identified specific actions the FEOC should take immediately and expand as time permits:

- Ensure there is space for several workstations to receive and coordinate inspection information, damage assessment information, logistics, and repair work.
- Have reliable communications with trade personnel in the field, vendors, consultants, engineers, and other departments and agencies. Communications equipment should consist of hard-wired telephones, FM radios, cellular phones, and email/texting capability. (Later the department would consider satellite phones and AM radios.)
- Have access to building record drawings commonly referred to "as-built drawings," utility maps, and Operations and Maintenance manuals.
- Maintain contact lists for university leaders, emergency personnel, vendors and suppliers, contractors, consultants, and governmental agencies.
- Obtain lists of personnel, students, staff, and faculty having disabilities and where they are located. This information must be treated as sensitive.

- Maintain equipment catalogs and other resources.
- Collect any standard operating procedures that have been developed.
- Maintain utility information such as contacts during an emergency, account numbers, and location of data files.

Frank knew that communication capability prior to, during, and after an emergency was essential for every possible emergency and emotional situation the department could encounter. He wanted a communication plan developed. However, he felt limited in his choices of the best person to lead this effort. Perhaps Bill Heard, the resource manager, could take it on; Bill was oriented toward technology, knew all the managers, and knew the university. So Frank asked Bill if he could develop the department communications plan. Bill was absolutely sure he could lead the effort and appreciated the trust Frank had demonstrated. Bill also thought it would dovetail nicely with his work on the computer maintenance management system.

Frank was elated and told Bill he would provide him some guidance. At the end of the week, Frank met with Bill, George, and Paul Larson, the central shops manager. Frank told Bill he invited Paul because the undertaking was big and Bill would need help collecting information. He added that Paul had access to much of what Bill would need and knew many of the issues. Frank thought they seemed to be amicable and would work well together.

Frank then recommended that Bill break out the communication as:

- general,
- before the emergency,
- during the emergency, and
- after the emergency.

Frank told Bill that, at a minimum, information for general communication, which could be used by the FEOC, should include specific building/facility information about: alarm systems, underground storage tanks, high-voltage feeders, emergency generators, life safety systems, elevators, water valve locations, natural gas shutoff locations, potable water resources, equipment shutdown procedures, access control information, and hazardous materials.

Collectively, this information could be called facility intelligence. In fact, Frank suggested that in time they develop a Facility Intelligence Resource

Guide (FIRG) that would contain all this information in one document which could be made available electronically. Eventually, other items could be added, such as prewritten emergency announcements and information notices that could be sent to employees, families, staff, faculty, and students.

In addition, Frank suggested that Bill collaborate with his assistant Rona, who was already coordinating the department's policies and procedures. Together, they could develop a policy for a departmental newsletter—a short, one-page update containing pictures of employees at work and very short descriptions of their projects. A newsletter would provide an excellent way to communicate with many leaders throughout the university about the FM department's activities.

Communication before an emergency would include actions being taken to foster trust and build credibility, and undertaken by the work management center (a.k.a. FEOC). One essential item to include before a known emergency, such as a hurricane, is coordination with service vendors for the equipment that may be needed, such as trailer-mounted generators. Also, everyone in the department should understand that only the director, or the FM duty officer, should provide information to the university leadership. This will diminish the possibility of incorrect information being shared.

Frank asked about mass communication capability and was told there was none. He decided to meet with the utilities director, Bill Green, to discuss options. They met at the central utility plant. One option they came up with was to obtain and install a locomotive steam whistle on the central plant. This plant provides steam and chill water to most buildings in the university. A steam whistle could be mounted on the central plant roof and be activated from steam generated in the plant.

Frank and Bill contacted a company in Texas that made steam whistles for locomotives. The cost to fabricate and ship a solid brass whistle was $6,000. Frank contacted the director of security, Matt King, and asked if anyone had pursued some type of mass notification system to inform staff, faculty, students, and visitors of impending danger, such as a tornado. Matt said there had been a recent meeting to discuss mass notification.

Because the cost was so expensive, $250,000, the issue was tabled. Frank then told Matt about the option to install a steam whistle at a cost of $6,000. When activated, the entire university and local community would hear the steam whistle, which would mean to shelter in. Matt liked the idea and suggested he and Frank brief the senior VP and get permission to pursue the whistle option.

Frank explained that leadership requires **communication during an emergency.** Before information can be sent, it needs to be reviewed and approved within the department. Therefore, they would need to train all the managers and supervisors. Also, they needed a plan to support the University Command Operating Center, which might require moving furniture and installing equipment.

In turn, Frank explained, **communication after an emergency** should include convening a lessons-learned, after-action review meeting. The team should review its support and key issues. The focus should be on what went well, what did not go well, and what steps should be taken to improve. Frank told Bill to anticipate that emergency communications systems could fail and, therefore, to have contingency plans ready. There could be situations when current technological devices (cellular phones, tablets) or the Internet and WiFi are not available. He wanted Bill to explore what is required to obtain an amateur radio license (citizen band AM radio, or ham radio).

This technology uses 1950s tube technology and is more resilient to electronic magnetic pulse (EMP) interference. Frank thought that the Federal Emergency Management Agency (FEMA) and the Federal Communications Commission (FCC) created a protocol called Radio Amateur Civil Emergency Service (RACES) for this purpose. He suggested that Bill look into RACES and the possibility and cost of satellite phones.

Finally, Frank recommended the team explore how to better use existing technology and social media such as Facebook, LinkedIn, Twitter, and any other communications technology to provide support to the university and the public. He recognized this was a big endeavor, requiring significant time and research. But Frank gave Bill, along with Paul, encouragement and a vote of confidence, asking them to keep him updated.

After speaking with Bill and Paul, Frank began thinking about emergencies like fire or explosions and the Authority Having Jurisdiction (AHJ) who would respond. He knew the AHJ was a government representative, usually the fire department or police- it could also be someone from other agencies in government- charged with enforcing the life safety code. Frank immediately decided there should be a protocol outlining an AHJ policy, procedure, and responsibilities. He asked Rona to include this information in her development of the department policies and procedures. He also thought meeting with the Metropolitan Fire and Police Chiefs was important and asked Rona to schedule a luncheon with them.

Next, Frank thought about mitigation and business continuity. He knew from experience that mitigation was essential to minimize emergencies from occurring. He thought about strategies he could implement based on assessing risks and identifying hazards. He also knew he was limited on funding. He called together several key managers (George, Bill Heard, Jim Askew, and Paul Larson) to meet in his office, using his whiteboard to brainstorm ideas.

Eventually, they reduced their doodling and notes to seven mitigation strategies:

- Comply with local codes and ordinances to prevent the hazard from occurring.
- Limit the amount and size of the hazard. Develop procedures for the storage of hazardous materials and conduct building inspections to ensure compliance with codes.
- Know what type of hazardous materials we have, their location, and amount. Keep hazardous materials separated.
- Properly store hazardous materials to prevent release.
- Ensure hazardous materials neutralizing agents are available.
- Disseminate information concerning hazardous materials. This would tie in with Bill's communication plan.
- Reduce the potential cost of emergencies by preparing in advance. This requires a detailed emergency management plan and training.

Frank recognized these strategies would require consistent and constant emphasis and training of the staff to be observant and follow up. He added them to the training list and the change management plan. As Frank contemplated these mitigation strategies, he knew this would be another major effort. He reviewed his staff's commitments.

Rona was compiling standard operating procedures with the help of the managers and their monthly meetings. Bill was working on developing a plan for a new CMMS and was also working on the department communications plan. Jim Askew was working on developing the PM program and asset management plan. Perhaps, he reflected, Paul Larson could be the manager to take on the mitigation strategies prior to and during emergencies.

Frank met with Paul a few days later. Although he did not know Paul well, he decided this was an opportunity to get to know him and his ability. He asked Paul if he might be interested in developing mitigation strategies. Paul looked at Frank with question marks in his eyes and asked what this responsibility would involve.

Frank explained he wanted a manager to look at the mitigation strategies and focus on the survivability of the university's facilities during and after an emergency. He needed someone experienced who knew what to look for and to make recommendations concerning survivability improvements to those structures. Paul responded that not only could he do that, but also that he could use some of the guys in the shops to help. Paul thought this would be a good experience for them. Paul's enthusiastic response was contagious.

Frank then recommended that Paul inspect each building exterior with focus on windows, roofs, and lightning protection:

- Windows. Examine them by location (office, classroom, residential) and consider that glass can be shattered by heavy winds, causing shards of glass to become projectiles and cause injuries. Develop recommendations on possible solutions to minimize the projectiles.
- Roofs. Examine for recommended repairs or corrective actions. Also, examine roof drains and scuppers and recommend any corrective actions. Develop a list of actions that should be taken prior to an approaching storm. Add this list to the evolving FM Emergency Management Plan. Identify actions that could be covered by preventive maintenance. Coordinate with Jim Askew and ensure he includes appropriate actions in his PM program and asset database.
- Lightning protection. Make sure existing systems are properly grounded. If there is no protection, develop a cost to install.

Over the weekend, Frank thought about business continuity. He knew that, once an organization was in the recovery stage following a major emergency or disaster, the facility manager should focus on continuing with operations to support the university's mission. Business operations were dependent on the availability and operability of the university's facilities and physical plant. He knew from experience that implementing a business continuity plan would have to evolve through several stages.

1. Protecting university facilities by reducing the impact of the emergency. This could be done by ensuring all physical plant equipment was maintained and operated properly.
2. Identifying and maintaining resources and processes. This would mean identifying key suppliers, contractors, and shippers and ensuring support agreements were in place for them to continue providing needed support. Frank thought about another university that had a great emergency plan and support agreements, but they were all in the same geographic area. When a disastrous situation occurred, the suppliers and contractors were also overcome and could not meet their support requirements. As a result, the university had to contact suppliers and contractors 200 miles away. The university had no relationship with these companies and risked higher costs and less quality of resources.
3. In an emergency there could be a need for additional resources such as warehousing, office space, vehicle parking, catering, and general transportation to and from the university.
4. The facility management business continuity plan would have to consider and identify specific logistical issues of who, what, when, where, and how. Once damaged facilities were identified, damage assessment teams would be sent to inspect and evaluate for safety and to determine needed corrective work.

As Frank thought of all these issues, he knew there would be costs beyond his budget. He realized the university needed an emergency funding reserve for these types of emergencies. Getting senior leadership involved and committed would be critical to any business continuity initiative. He decided he would start to assemble a briefing to senior leaders, using as his main reference the National Fire Protection Association's NFPA 1600, *National Standard on Disaster and Emergency Management and Business Continuity*.

One evening as Frank arrived home, he received a text from Matt King, who was Frank's counterpart focused on security at the university. Matt was a retired Secret Service agent who had been the university's Director of Security for three years. Matt and Frank had a good relationship, and the FM department provided support to Matt's department when requested. Matt was concerned about a physical security threat he had been briefed on by the Metropolitan Police. He wanted to meet with Frank early the next morning to discuss Crime Prevention through Environmental Design (CPTED).

When they met, Matt explained CPTED as a concept that focuses on four strategies: natural surveillance, natural access control, territorial reinforcement, and maintenance. Matt had read Randall Atlas' book, *21st Century Security and CPTED*, and was focused on the maintenance strategy. He wanted to ensure that shrubbery and tree limbs were trimmed away from perimeter light poles and building lights.

Matt was concerned that cameras installed at strategic locations could not distinguish unfriendly and possible hostile activity. Frank indicated his appreciation and stated he would have his grounds folks jump on this immediately. Frank understood the importance of physical security and was concerned about complacency becoming a physical security challenge.

As Frank was departing, he asked Matt if he or one of his officers could teach a class to the FM department about CPTED and the National Incident Management System (NIMS). NIMS is a security system established to improve coordination between government agencies and the private sector to prevent, respond to, and recover from various emergencies. Frank felt strongly that everyone in FM should understand what NIMS is and when it should be implemented. Matt agreed with Frank that a special class was a great idea and they would be happy to teach it.

Chapter Fourteen
Measuring

Point To Ponder: To improve operations, maintenance, and service: Measure, measure, measure! Then verify and analyze.

One morning, George came into Frank's office and wanted to talk. He was working on his MBA through the university. He told Frank that the professor in his management class had discussed the importance of measuring what the organization does and comparing those measures to an established baseline. The professor focused on total quality management (TQM) and the need for continuous improvement.

George commented that the FM department was not measuring anything; he questioned how they would ever improve what they did. George added that most employees considered their jobs as a necessity because they were paid well and needed a job. Otherwise, they have no allegiance to the university.

Frank contemplated George's comments for a minute, then stated his agreement. In order to benchmark the FM department with other universities, Frank asked George to check with several associations, including the Association of Higher Education Facility Officers (known as APPA), the International Facility Management Association (IFMA), and the Association for Facilities Engineering (AFE).

They could have information or reports the department could use. This conversation took place on Tuesday. Frank asked if George could check these associations and be ready to discuss by Friday. George responded that he would give it a shot.

On Friday morning George and Frank met again. George had contacted all three associations and learned they all had reports and measurement statistics the FM department could obtain since they were already members. Frank told George to go ahead and obtain the benchmark reports. Then he shared another idea. He suggested they pick a half dozen universities the university measured itself against.

After the spring semester ended, Frank wanted George to schedule visits to each one, to meet with their FM leaders and collect information they could use as benchmarks, such as:

- Cost per square foot to maintain facilities,
- Amount of square footage maintained by each trade,
- Amount of square footage cleaned per custodian,
- Workforce productivity,
- The ratio of planned maintenance to reactive maintenance,
- Utility cost per square foot, and
- Average completion and response time per work order.

More items would likely be added by the time George made his visits. But, as Frank pointed out, they needed to ensure that whatever they benchmarked with their university partners involved matching "apples to apples." It seemed they had the beginnings of a benchmarking program.

Frank knew the importance of measuring what the department does. He wanted to find better ways for Operations and Maintenance to support the university. He realized benchmarking was of tremendous value when measuring performance as it relates to other universities. The process could be a motivator to improve the capabilities of the department, but first they had to understand the difference in application and cost, and what needed to be done to improve operations and maintenance support.

Benchmarking would enable the department to capture the best practices from those selected universities and then consider implementing those practices within the FM department. Frank could also use the benchmarking data when he gave briefings to the university leadership. Using this data would help him show what the department was measuring and also demonstrate trends for improving. This alone could help him obtain funding for additional projects he wanted to accomplish.

Frank was also concerned with quality management. He knew that customers (internal employees and external staff, faculty, and students) defined the quality of service based on their expectations and perceptions. Benchmarking could help explain why certain actions were taken, and also illustrate improvement trends within the department. In addition to benchmarking, Frank wanted George to explore using key performance indicators (KPIs). KPIs are metrics which measure how well the organization is achieving its goals and objectives. Specifically, Frank wanted to know the state of deferred maintenance (increasing, remaining the same, or decreasing), and the state of reactive maintenance in relation to the PM program. These could be used to compare actual results against the expected results of the KPIs.

Lastly, when George visited the universities, Frank suggested he find out what they did well—their best practices that the FM department could adopt. George was unclear what Frank meant by best practices. Frank responded that they were approaches and methods that proved to be successful and effective accomplishing the mission of achieving quality service. He added that by the time George conducted his visits, they may have developed some of their own best practices he could share with the other universities. Frank summarized their discussion, telling George, **"We have to measure what we do, market what we do, and communicate what we do."**

Chapter Fifteen
Design and Engineering

Point To Ponder: Understand how projects are initiated, designers selected, contracts administered, work inspected, and documents archived

Frank also took time to meet with other department heads, including the director of design and engineering, the director of administration and budget, and the director of utilities. He was anxious to understand how capital projects were initiated, designers selected, construction contracts administered, contract work inspected, and documents archived for future reference.

He knew from experience that it took one to three years for a major capital project to be programmed, planned, designed, constructed, and commissioned. On very large projects, it could take even longer. He also wanted to learn about the space inventory—its allocation, forecasting, and management. Having learned that design and engineering held weekly meetings to review projects, Frank decided to attend them.

This would provide an opportunity to get to know all ten project managers and the potential problems with each ongoing project; those problems could ultimately impact operations and maintenance of that facility. He also wanted to know the archivist for design and engineering. The archives contained all the past and present building designs, record drawings (sometimes called "as-built" drawings), operations and maintenance manuals, warranties, and contracts for various projects.

As-built drawings are critical to be kept up to date, especially when equipment is being replaced or when major renovations are ongoing. Hence, the archivist plays a key role to ensure that contractors—even in-house maintenance personnel—keep these drawings updated with the latest information. Past practices reveal that changes are usually shown in red ink on the actual drawing so they can be easily seen during a review. Today, most paper drawings are digitized, which will benefit the department in the future. Frank knew the archives would be important to his department when it came to future emergencies. He made a note that Jim Askew should coordinate often with the archivist concerning the asset management plan. Whenever key pieces of equipment are replaced, an annotation should be made on the record drawing.

As Frank was speaking with several project managers, he overheard a discussion concerning an ongoing construction project. The contractor had submitted a request for substitution of a piece of equipment and the project manager was considering approving. Frank couldn't help himself. He chimed in that substitution should never be allowed unless reasonable payment credit is given by the contractor. His experience was that contractors seldom want to credit the payments when they make substitutions. He told the project managers they may also see a contractor specify that a piece of equipment to be installed is approved equals, which really means cheaper.

Frank obtained a list of new ongoing capital construction projects. He decided to walk through the projects with each project manager. As he had done within his department, to understand issues and get to know individuals (MBWA), he wanted to know the project managers and understand their strengths, weaknesses, and challenges. He knew from past experience that turnover of design, engineering, and construction projects did not always go smoothly. Designers and contractors were interested in completing the project, even though there may be issues from an O&M standpoint on how to maintain projects being turned over.

Frank reflected on a project from his past. He was walking through the lobby and atrium of a newly constructed building with the design engineer and the project manager. In the atrium, he looked up toward the skylights, about 60 feet high, and saw lights at the top, along the wall around the atrium. He asked the project manager and designer how they were supposed to change out the lights. The flippant answer he received from the designer was, "That's your problem to figure out."

Frank knew he would have to rent or purchase some type of articulating lift that could reach at least 60 feet, and also fit through the lobby entrance doors. This was a cost he was not aware of and had not considered it in his budget. Frank learned a valuable lesson that he never forgot. He determined that, from then on, he would be intimately involved with the planning and design of major projects. He resolved that O&M had to have a say in what was designed, how it was installed, and how it was turned over for Operations and Maintenance.

He remembered an experience where a senior manager within an academic department hired a contractor to renovate a portion of the building, but never informed the FM department. The contractor installed new electrical circuits and did not identify the circuits in the electrical panel. When a FM electrician was performing an electrical PM, he went to the panel and noticed the new unmarked circuits. He then reported this to his immediate manager who informed Frank. Frank contacted the senior manager and in a calm manner explained that all work had to be requested by submitting a work order, which enabled work to be tracked and properly identified. Frank further explained that bypassing this process could have serious ramifications, resulting in injury or code violations which could result in expensive fines.

Frank had another thought and told the director of design and engineering that O&M also needed to be involved with developing the final project punch list and signing off on the list. As a project comes to an end, a list is compiled naming deficiencies, items requiring immediate attention, and items not conforming to the contract specifications. In both smaller and million-dollar projects, a punch list can have hundreds of items requiring correction—sometimes thousands in larger projects. These items must be corrected or completed by the contractor before final payment is made and the project turned over for Operations and Maintenance.

The term *punch list* comes from a historical administrative process of punching a hole in the document list, next to one of the items on the list. Punching indicated that the work was completed for that particular construction task. Frank told the director of design and engineering that either he or one of his managers would be involved with final inspections and signing off the items on the punch list.

One of the larger capital projects was an addition to an existing building. This multimillion-dollar project had structural, mechanical, electrical, and fire system installations. Based on his experience, Frank asked about commissioning of the project; he understood commissioning was a tool that should be used to obtain a quality project. He knew that a commissioning agent is an independent authority who provides expertise to verify that all systems installed work as intended.

The project manager gave Frank a complete rundown of the project and introduced him to the commissioning agent. Again, Frank asked questions and focused specifically on the end-of-project training for his staff: when was it to be scheduled, who should attend, what systems would be trained on, and who would conduct the training? The project manager indicated the project was due to be completed in the next two weeks, and training would be conducted around that time. Frank stated he wanted to attend; furthermore, he wanted the training videotaped for future reference by technicians.

Frank asked one final question about attic stock. One of the junior project managers who heard the question asked Frank what attic stock was. Frank explained it was a percentage of project material—such as carpeting, floor tile, and paint—that is left with the O&M department in case material had to be replaced or repaired in the future. The term *attic stock* came when this extra material was stored in the attic of the building. The project manager then told Frank there would be 10 percent left at the end of the project. The remaining question was where it would be stored.

Chapter Sixteen
Sustainability

Point To Ponder: FM is the steward of sustainable practices

Frank was receiving phone calls and queries from students as well as some faculty concerning their interest in sustainability. They were requesting the university leadership to endorse sustainability by promoting high performance, healthful, energy-efficient, and environmentally safe buildings and grounds. Even Frank's boss, Steve Smith, was asking him what he could do to support the students.

Frank wanted the department to be known as the stewards of the environment, so he discussed the issue with several managers, including the landscape and grounds manager. Frank had some initial thoughts but wanted to hear from the managers. After all, they needed to be invested with any sustainability decision if they were to support it fully. Frank posed the question to the managers and waited for their ideas to generate.

Immediately, the landscape and grounds manager, Chris Philpot, offered a suggestion. He indicated that on the far side of the football field there was a grounds storage area approximately a half-acre in size. He suggested that some of that space could be used by students for composting or student gardens. Frank thought this was a relatively simple sustainable idea that would be inexpensive to implement; it would also demonstrate the department's support for sustainability. He decided to go forward with that recommendation.

Chris then chimed in again with another suggestion—to expand the recycling operation. He said they already recycle now, but maybe could push it more. He suggested more advertising with signage and Web postings, and perhaps getting students more involved.

Other managers began to make suggestions as well. These included solar panel installation, changing to LED lights, switching to green chemicals for cleaning and industrial use, and using bio-digestive enzymes for digesting grease in the kitchens. All of these suggestions were doable and relatively inexpensive to implement. Frank asked George to meet with the student group and discuss installing solar panels. He further suggested selecting one of the university's off-campus townhouses as a possibility. If the students agreed, then Frank would approach the leadership with a plan for solar panel installation.

Paul Larson, the central shops manager, suggested the FM department conduct an energy audit, starting with one building. He thought they may be able to do it with his folks in the shops. The audit could point out which energy systems are leaking energy and causing them to waste money. Then, if this first effort proved successful, they could expand to other buildings. This would give their tradespeople an opportunity to put their training to work. It would also demonstrate interest in the environment. As a bonus, they could add the repair or replacement of equipment to the O&M plan.

Frank summarized the discussions, complimenting all the great ideas and suggestions that need to be shared. He expressed thanks for their participation and interest. He noted how much the FM department could do if everyone thought outside the box and communicated with each other. Following the meeting, Frank prepared a short electronic report which he sent to his boss. The report summarized the meeting and suggestions. He also stated that he was preparing a presentation.

Later in the afternoon, his boss called him regarding sustainability and explained that the university leadership planned to pursue Leadership in Energy and Environmental Design (LEED) certification of the U.S. Green Building Council for its next capital project. LEED certification ranged from high to low: platinum, gold, silver, and bronze. Steve also wanted to know if the newest residence hall could be certified as LEED Gold using the LEED-EBOM (Leadership in Energy and Environmental Design of Existing Building Operations and Maintenance) certification process. Frank responded affirmatively but indicated additional funding would be required.

When Steve asked why, Frank explained there were specific requirements to achieve LEED certification. These had to be documented and meet the established criteria, such as changing HVAC filters at the prescribed interval. Also, all the maintenance concerning sustainability had to be documented in order to recertify the facility in five years. These requirements were not being met at the time because there were neither enough staff to do the work nor the proper supplies because of budget reductions.

Frank emphasized that sustainability concerning LEED certification was doable, but there was a cost. Additionally, as new buildings were certified, there was a documentation requirement for recertification years into the future. As an example, he told Steve that certifying a building as LEED platinum or gold was great, but these buildings may or may not be recertified in the future. Finally, Frank summarized that he and his staff would do what they could concerning LEED building certification. They would also work with the student groups on the suggestions he described earlier.

Chapter Seventeen
Monthly Updates

Point To Ponder: Keep the "boss" informed

Frank provided his boss with short monthly updates about his activities. These were simple email summaries, usually two to three pages in length, but sometimes longer, depending on the issue. Some memos he called his "think pieces" where he offered recommendations on various FM issues. Frank learned from previous experience that to be successful one has to "keep the boss informed." To Frank that meant understanding what is expected and furnishing information to provide his boss with a "warm comfortable feeling" that he knew what he was doing.

Toward the end of the six months, Frank summarized all the areas on which he focused. This was a lengthy paper, 15 pages. In it, he also listed areas of concern that had to be addressed, along with his thoughts about the future of the organization, and how the department should organize to better support the university. The summary of areas on which Frank focused is shown below. There were so many areas that he could not completely prioritize them. He also mentioned that tackling each of these issues would require consistency; it will be a long-term process.

At the end of each issue, Frank listed the name of the individual responsible for follow-up:

- Meeting with department managers and foremen. Get to know them as individuals, and their strengths and weaknesses. Scheduled daily

8:00 A.M. meetings. (Frank)

- Reviewed night maintenance support. Understand who the technicians are and what they do. Start reviewing the options to provide more coverage. (Frank)
- Reviewed the preventive maintenance program. Understand who manages the program, the size of the program, how preventive maintenance work orders are issued, and the completion rate. (Jim)
- Reviewed asset management and determined a plan was needed to get it moving. (Jim)
- Asked to see the department vision, mission, and goals. Was told that there was none. Began discussion on developing and implementing. (Frank)
- Was told by the HR Vice President to dust off the union labor strike plan, but it did not exist. Started researching and developing a plan. (Frank)
- Reviewed the budget and learned the current existing procedures to develop the FM budget. (Bill and Frank)
- Met most employees, one-on-one. Learned that all the employees liked working Monday through Friday, 7:30 A.M. to 4:00 P.M., which needs to be reconsidered since the university operates 24/7/365. (Frank)
- Reviewed and discussed the training program. Found there is limited and minimal ongoing training, and no budget line item to fund. Initiated the beginning of a training plan. (Rona)
- Reviewed and discussed ongoing and planned Operations and Maintenance projects. (Frank)
- Reviewed the procurement process for supplies and services. (Bob and Ed)
- Reviewed and discussed existing service contracts. Met with leaders of each contract. (Frank and Ed)
- Reviewed and discussed policies and standard operating procedures. Found that very few existed. Started process to develop. (George and Rona)
- Reviewed and discussed how work requests are received and processed. Learned how work requests are entered into Excel spreadsheets as work orders, assigned to shops and zones, completed, and

closed out. Anticipate the need for a computer maintenance management system (CMMS). (Bill)

- Reviewed and discussed measuring, including benchmarking information and key performance indicators (KPIs). Started developing a plan. (George and Bill)
- Met with design and engineering staff to understand how capital projects are developed and managed. Sat in some of the ongoing weekly project review meetings. Also, attended end-of-project training for technicians. (Frank)
- Reviewed the department emergency management plan, including communications. Found it to be minimal and in need of expansion. (Frank and Bill)
- Discussed and started the process to develop a communications plan. (Bill)
- Discussed sustainability projects and provided recommendations to students. (George)
- Met with the Metropolitan Fire and Police Chiefs whose departments support the university. These organizations are the Authorities Having Jurisdiction with which the FM department is primarily involved. Scheduled a cookout so managers could also meet the chiefs and their key subordinates. (Frank)

PART II DISCUSSION QUESTIONS

1. Why should a facility management organization have a vision, a mission statement, and goals?

2. To change the organization, where should Frank begin?

3. What is organizational culture? How can it be changed?

4. Is preventive maintenance critical for the FM department? How does the FM ensure it is completed?

5. When should preventive maintenance be accomplished?

6. How should after-hours maintenance be handled?

7. Should FM department plan for staffing 24/7/365?

8. Why is communication important? How should FM managers communicate?

9. What are the mitigation strategies?

10. Does the FM manager need a management philosophy, and should it be publicized?

11. Do you have and know your policies and procedures? Why is this important or not important?

12. Why is benchmarking important? KPIs?

13. Why are as-builts, punch lists, and commissioning important to understand?

PART THREE
THE FIRST YEAR

Chapter Eighteen
A Decision

Point To Ponder: Start with the basics

Frank contemplated the events, issues, and people he had experienced during his first six months in his position. He knew the demand on his time, in the future, would be significant. He also knew that he had amassed a wealth of knowledge and now had to devise a plan to tackle all the issues. He thought this plan could take many years of consistent and dedicated effort.

He reflected on his first day on the job and the carpenter shop foreman's comment that the managers and foremen were taking bets he would not last a year. Was it really worth it? His passion was operations and maintenance, and he loved a challenge, but this experience was different from earlier ones.

Previously, he experienced challenges and knew that, at most, he would have to endure three years. After that, he would be reassigned to another position and task. Now it was different. Either he produced and succeeded or he moved to another job. That's what happened to the previous six directors. Apparently, they came to the same conclusion and decided to leave. Hence, the department was in chaos and turmoil.

Frank decided to discuss his thoughts with his wife. He knew she had to be invested with whatever decision he made. In the past, she accepted his long hours at work and his deployments for weeks and months at a time. But they both had longed to be together more. Frank's wife told him she would support whatever decision he made.

After much contemplation, Frank decided he would take on this challenge. At least he would be going home every night and seeing the family. In addition, he would be doing something he wanted to do. He thought he could make an impact and help people.

As Frank reflected on his years of experience and the many leadership books and challenges he had studied, he considered that leaders cannot afford to bungle. They had to lead and inspire. But what did that really mean in his current situation? It meant displaying his experience and knowledge, portraying an air of confidence, being determined and decisive, and developing a vision for the department. All of these traits would help him cultivate employee trust in him.

Because of the number of significant issues in the department, Frank knew success would require a balancing act. He would have to attack numerous issues concurrently and consistently. He decided he would continue to assign projects to his deputy, George. They had a good working relationship and had developed trust and confidence with each other. Frank could use George as a sounding board for his ideas.

Frank reviewed the department issues he had studied over the last six months. He knew that facility management must keep its facilities safe, healthy, and in proper operating condition. The facilities must meet the needs of the people who occupy them.

Next, Frank listed the issues the department faced:

- The lackadaisical attitude of some FM employees he encountered,
- Lack of strategic and tactical planning to develop projects which ultimately impact the budget,
- Minimal policies and procedures,
- Insufficient training because there is no budget line for funding,
- Very little asset management capability because of limited automation availability,
- No effective emergency management plan and no overall communications strategy, and
- No ability to measure how the department compares with other similar organizations and how customers perceive the service they receive.

Based on these issues, Frank concluded, and told George, that the department needs to integrate the basics of what it does into everything it plans for the future before it can advance.

George asked what the basics were on which they needed to focus.

Frank responded with the following priorities, saying they needed to tie in with their vision, mission, and goals:

- Quality management and customer service
- Professionalism
- Communication and marketing
- Develop relationships
- Measure what we do
- Manage our space
- Understand and develop our facility intelligence
- Implement and expand asset management and preventive maintenance
- Expand our training program
- Focus on physical security
- Continue developing and implementing policies and procedures
- Develop a strong emergency management plan

Chapter Nineteen
Facility Management Strategy

Point To Ponder: Develop a plan of action to achieve established goals

In many one-on-one discussions with George, Frank expressed his frustration of not having a strategy to attack and navigate through all the issues encountered within the department. When George asked him what he meant by "strategy," Frank explained that a strategy was a plan of action to achieve established goals. He added that, at that moment, they didn't really know where they were going, comparing it to driving a car with a blindfold on.

Frank and George concluded they needed a facility management strategy. They decided to start by developing the department vision, mission, and goals, which they both considered important tools to shape that strategy. Frank suggested that, before they could take on that task, they needed to understand the overall university business plan, which included the university's vision for the future, its stated mission, and its established values. Therefore, he would first meet with his boss and the senior VP to get a better understanding of where the university was going.

When Frank and George met again a few days later, Frank explained what he learned about the university business plan. He stated they were on the right path. He also knew if he and George developed the department's vision, mission, and goals on their own, these would be perceived as theirs instead of the department's. The managers and foremen had to be involved, especially with developing the objectives to achieve each goal.

One of Frank's favorite sayings was *"everyone has to be invested."* The objectives are the essential "nitty-gritty" of how to begin achieving the goals—where facility action plans begin coming into play, along with important aspects of strategic planning (long-range, mid-range, and annual work plans). Eventually, operating plans, policies, and procedures are developed and implemented as the vehicles to convert plans into action.

A format and recommended list of policies and procedures had been developed by Rona King. The monthly meetings with managers had started to produce some departmental policies and standard maintenance procedures. Because policies focus on organizational issues and activities, George had many coordination challenges, which took time. Many of the policies involved employees; as a result, the HR department and the legal office would play a significant role. Stakeholders, health and safety representatives, and contractors who worked for the university also had to be consulted. Additionally, the union had to be involved.

Developing the specific procedures were a little easier since they focused on how selected activities should be done. Once approved as standard, maintenance, or emergency, each procedure would then be consolidated into the department's overall operating procedures. The key was that both the policies and procedures had to be easy to understand and apply.

Developing policies and procedures can be challenging, yet relatively easy overall. They also need to be synchronized with the department vision, mission, and goals. Frank realized that implementation and compliance were going to be major hurdles. To be effective, the policies and procedures had to be coordinated. Therefore, all managers, supervisors, foremen, and employees had to be involved. Once developed and approved, the policies and procedures needed to be made available to the entire workforce.

Training would be needed on each. Frank wanted everyone to sign that they read, understood, and would comply with the policies and procedures. He asked Rona to make a short summary of each policy and procedure, then provide a copy to everyone in the department. He also asked Rona to establish a review cycle of each on a two-year cycle. The purpose of the review cycle would be to determine if the policies and procedures were still functioning properly and as intended, or if they should be revised or updated.

Because of reduced funding and limited staff, Frank knew that emergencies would start to become the norm. The department's operations and maintenance strategy would have to include an emphasis on emergency response. Specific plans would be needed for the types of emergencies that could occur. These would include hazardous materials spills, fire protection, emergency communications, storm preparedness (including snow events), workplace violence, electrical power failures, indoor air quality, infectious disease, physical security, water disruption, and terrorism. Concurrently the department had to consider quality management to ensure customer satisfaction.

Frank thought of water disruption and an incident that he previously experienced and shared it with George. The local water treatment facility that provided water to his facility had to be shut down due to possible water contamination. Frank was informed that water was being shut off that evening. He was concerned because he had several thousand people living and working in this facility. He knew they would need potable water to drink and he had to consider toilet facilities. He and several of his subordinates began calling water distribution companies. By 7 P.M. that day they had 50,000 gallons of potable bottled water being shipped to his installation. It was due to begin arriving starting at 5 A.M. the next day.

Frank also had his managers coordinate for individual portable toilets and trailers. Also, since they had access to the gymnasium pool Frank planned to move pool water in 50-gallon containers to the occupied buildings. The containers would be transported using department pickup trucks and delivered to the building lobbies. Occupants needing to use first-floor toilets could pick up a bucket of water for flushing.

The next morning the palletized bottled water began arriving in tractor trailers. Frank had personnel and equipment available to unload the water and store it in a large tent used for special events. Since it was winter, and the temperature was in the 20s and 30s the tent had to be heated. Frank asked Bob Brown to rent salamander heaters for the tent. Concurrently, the individual portable toilets and trailers began arriving. The pickup trucks began hauling gym swimming pool water to the buildings.

Two days later the water treatment plant spokesperson contacted Frank and stated the water contamination problem was corrected and water distribution was beginning. Now Frank could return the portable toilets and trailers. His department could stop hauling water to the building lobbies for the first floor toilets. But what was he to do with the remaining 45,000 gallons of bottled water? His solution was to give away as much as possible and store the remainder in a large mechanical room until it could be used in the kitchen and dining area. Not great solutions, but at least he had a plan. As Frank reviewed this incident, he decided to task George to meet with the managers and begin developing a water disruption emergency management plan.

Chapter Twenty
Change Management

Point To Ponder: Consistent communication and empathetic listening leads to success

Change in a university workplace requires planning, consistency, and daily emphasis because it involves employees, students, tenants, staff, faculty, customers, parents, and visitors. The impact on employees includes changes in organization structure, human resource issues, cultural issues, technology, and budgets. Change in the FM department involves changing the way the organization operates. To Frank, this meant FM employees would need to let go of old ways of performing work and responding to work requests. It would mean changing habits.

Frank knew that change evolves through stages of resistance. His experience identified that most change efforts fail because information is not communicated to staff, customers, and other interested parties on a consistent basis. Open, sincere communication is essential to begin cultivating credibility and trust. Every possible communication channel should be used, including newsletters, weekly notes, town hall meetings, and a dedicated website. For change to be effective, there has to be positive, continuous reinforcement and feedback. In addition, there has to be ongoing leadership training for the managers, supervisors, and foremen.

In discussions with various leaders within the university—including department chairs and deans—Frank deduced that change initiatives were taking place throughout. The university had taken a positive step forward in change management by realizing that, as the university grew, the FM department would need to be able to maintain the facilities and grounds. As the maintenance improved, students would become prouder of their institution. In turn, this pride would eventually translate into alumni who donate to their alma mater.

Frank knew employees would resist changes if they perceived the changes would impact them in a negative way. For example, employees would focus on unfavorable outcomes such as less money or personal inconvenience. Some employees would not want to break established habits. Emotions and feelings would be expressed forcefully and were to be expected.

Frank had experience with change management in his previous career. He knew that people internalize change in different ways. Some people don't accept change and, therefore, cannot function; they often become depressed. Others get angry at supervisors, managers, and the organization in general. Some just tolerate the change and do their job but are apathetic.

Taking this into consideration, Frank said to George, "Everyone should understand that the benefits of change will occur only when employees understand the changes being made, why they are being made, know the timeline, and are supportive of the department's vision, mission, goals, and values. Hence, we have to have good, constant communication."

After much thought and discussion with George, Frank decided to start by meeting with subordinate managers and supervisors first. He would listen to them, be enthusiastic, and learn their input, ideas, and recommendations. He knew there would have to be compromise. Frank had been practicing being an active and empathetic listener. He wanted the managers to recognize that he was trying to see things and understand from their perspective. He also was watching each of the managers and supervisors for nonverbal cues to indicate whether they were receptive, open, or totally against the change being discussed. Once these managers and supervisors understood and supported the resultant changes because they participated and were invested in the changes, they could assist by speaking with their employees.

Frank knew he had to continue building trust and credibility with everyone in the department. He thought he could do this by being open-minded, transparent, and patient—listening to employees making presentations or asking questions and providing clear explanations. This is where his courses in communications would come in. Although he had initially thought those courses were a waste of his time, he had learned through trial and error that communication was the path to success and listening was the most important aspect.

At the start of this process, he initiated a survey to be completed by all employees. He did the same for stakeholders. This initial survey would become the baseline to measure how the ongoing change process was working. He planned to conduct an updated survey periodically, perhaps quarterly. This process would provide a means of measuring how change was being accepted.

Much communication would be needed to help employees change their habits. The HR department and union representatives would be invited to assist during group discussions, even in private meetings. Frank also planned to brief the union representatives, separately, on proposed changes and solicit their support. Frank asked George to develop a list of expectations that employees would be required to meet, which included: absenteeism, reporting to work on time, shift hours, etc. Frank planned to meet with employees and share this list. Then he would meet with each employee and ask them to sign the list; this policy tool would be valuable and become a contract between the employee and the department.

Frank decided to implement a Facility Management-Stakeholder Service Council (FMSSC) consisting of other department heads such as health and environmental safety, human resources, public safety, and risk management. He felt that he could not lead the FM department through the change process without the support of other departments that had experienced change and believed in the cause. This council would also function as a process action oversight committee. It would meet quarterly, provide updates to the leadership on the status of changes, and keep employees updated on the status of the changes.

To be effective, the change effort would need to be carefully explained and updates delivered to the entire FM department on a routine basis, by both written communication and leadership discussions and actions. Additionally, a monthly newsletter (distributed to employees with copies to stakeholders) would be established. Frank placed Rona in charge of developing the newsletter and ensuring it was distributed to all employees. Quarterly town hall meetings would also be scheduled.

As part of the change effort, a policy and procedure update would have to accompany every change adopted. Frank knew this would require someone to make the required changes and ensure these approved changes were communicated to all employees and key stakeholders within the university. Frank decided that George should take on this responsibility.

Based on his previous experience, Frank believed in after-action reviews, better known as lessons learned. He knew no matter how successful the change effort was, there were always things that could make the process work better in the future. It was up to him to ensure that the lessons learned were identified, discussed, and documented.

He decided that a permanent record of the change process should include an analysis of what worked and what didn't. He wanted everything documented because it enabled the entire process to be replicated, and it would be transparent. Finally, he wanted someone to capture process notes and then prepare an outline and summary that would help team members write their "lessons learned." These lessons learned would be published in a newsletter every quarter. He tapped Rona for this.

Chapter Twenty-one
Vision, Mission, Goals

Point To Ponder: Vision, mission, and goals provide direction to the organization

Frank understood every organization should have its own vision and mission statements and a list of goals it intended to address in support of the parent organization. This seemed like an insignificant task, which could be done quickly; however, if it were to be done properly, both Frank and George knew it would take time and require assistance. A good department vision, mission, and goals would provide a direction on how to support the overall institution. They would have dramatic positive influence over the service support provided to the university. They would also help the department become more customer-focused, effective, and cost-efficient.

Frank knew it was important for the director to hold meetings with employees, to explain the intent to develop the department vision, mission, and goals, and to solicit their involvement. To manage possible conflict that might evolve with employees, supervisors, and management, there should be a facilitation process. The first attempt would be taken by Frank, who would make every effort to resolve the issue at the lowest level. If Frank needed assistance, then the facilitation process could be implemented.

A facilitation process is a method of having someone who is completely neutral and knowledgeable about group dynamics keep the group and agenda on track by involving the director, managers, and supervisors and ensuring decisions are made in an autonomous and uncensored way. George mentioned that consideration should be given to using someone from the human resources department or the Business and Management School as a facilitator. This method would involve encouraging people to participate in the process of exchanging information and ideas so they become invested in what is discussed and decided. Frank thought that was a great idea and contacted the vice president of human resources and the dean of Business and Management School to get their input to this concept.

Frank and George then developed and decided on the following explanations to help with developing the department vision, mission, goals, and objectives:

1. The FM department should have a vision as to what it would like to achieve in support of the university. This vision is a dream statement summarizing where the organization is heading. The intent is to turn the dream into a reality. The vision must be clear, relevant, and achievable; otherwise, confusion will occur and the vision will not be accepted.

2. The mission is a general statement of how the FM department will achieve its organization vision. The FM mission statement should focus on describing the reason for the FM department to exist and how the vision will be accomplished.

3. Goals are realistic general statements of what the FM department wants to achieve to meet its mission. More specifically, goals are milestones in the process of implementing a strategy. Each goal has someone assigned to manage it, provide periodic updates, and coordinate the objectives. A target date is established for the completion of the goal. This date is flexible and can be adjusted based on the current situation and difficulty.

4. Objectives provide implementation steps and a specific timeline for achieving each goal. Each objective turns a goal's general statement of what is to be accomplished into a specific, measurable statement of when and how it will be achieved. This entire effort involves people and change; therefore, patience, consistency, and persistence are especially important.

5. Values depict how members of the organization will behave during the process of establishing the FM department vision, mission, goals,

and objectives. Some values which can be exemplified and considered include professionalism, respect for individuals, integrity, dedication to work, excellence in everything done, innovation, teamwork, adaptability to customer needs, exceptional service, honesty, empowerment, communication, and stewardship.

The explanations that Frank and George developed would play an important role related to the department's success. They would provide the department's destination—the direction for the department to follow—and align the resources to achieve success.

Chapter Twenty-two
The Plan

Point To Ponder: Developing the plan takes time and consistent effort

Frank pondered his method for "Plan Development." He decided to bring in a consultant he knew, someone who had helped him develop a change management strategy a few years earlier. He intended to have the consultant help him and his managers develop the initial department vision, mission, goals, and objectives using the explanations he and George defined.

Then he would present it to the employees to get their involvement, and then adjust as needed. Over a period of two months, the consultant, along with Frank and all the managers—a total of 15 people—met one day a week for four hours. They crafted a mission statement, a vision of where the department was going, goals to achieve the vision, and objectives to achieve each goal.

Once completed, Frank briefed his boss, university leaders, and union representatives. He wanted everyone's buy-in. Of course, there were many questions and also objections from the union representatives. Each issue was discussed, explanations provided, and, in some cases, modifications made. The one major objection by the union representatives addressed the change of work hours. Frank knew from his first six months that the department's work hours of 7:30 A.M. to 4:00 P.M., Monday through Friday, were not going to be sufficient to support a growing and expanding university. This was especially true since more than 10,000 students lived on campus and classes were held until 10:00 P.M. and on weekends. He felt there should be coverage on 24/7/365. Many of his managers thought the same.

In addition, Frank thought that some PM work orders could and should be performed after normal work hours. By coverage, he thought of the myriad types of issues that can occur: HVAC failures, elevator problems, loss of electrical power, fire alarm and sprinkler activations, indoor air quality issues, floods, etc. Following a series of meetings with the union, HR, and the legal team they came to an agreement on how best to proceed. The department would develop work shifts covering 24/7/365, along with the required number of employees per shift. Some shifts would cover 8 hours, some would cover 12 hours, and some shifts would be filled with part-time positions covering 16 hours on weekends. All 300 employees would be asked to fill out a card with their first, second, and third shift priority.

Once all the shifts and the number of employees per shift were identified, Frank asked George to call an all-hands meeting for everyone in the department. Frank knew the department would have to go through a review process with the employees. He wanted to begin the process by focusing on the draft vision, mission, goals, objectives, and values. He wanted to get the employees involved!

The employees certainly did get involved. Frank had to muster all his patience to listen to employee complaints, then calmly and carefully explain the department's future. There were many questions about potential layoffs, pay, overtime, and incentive pay. Employee comments were reviewed and carefully considered; some were implemented. Once modifications were made, Frank called another all-hands meeting.

Once they understood the reason for the change, the employees were given cards that identified the various shifts they could select as their number one, two, or three priority. They were given a week to think about it, discuss it with family members, and ask questions. The following week, George collected the cards from the supervisors and managers. Then Frank, George, and Rona laid out the completed cards. To their surprise, out of 300 employee cards, only one person did not get the first or second shift he wanted. That person decided to leave the university.

All the other employees received their first or second choice. Interestingly, there were three trade technicians who selected the evening shift, Tuesday through Friday, 11:00 A.M. to 9:30 P.M. At first, they complained about having selected that shift, but after a few weeks they loved it and were very supportive of the change. All three lived 60 miles from the university. Because of the new schedule, they missed traffic coming to work and had no traffic going home. They also had a three-day weekend every week.

Once the cards were reviewed and organized by shift, a string of small townhall meetings were scheduled where employees could ask questions. After the initial meetings had taken place, Frank decided to schedule similar sessions with customers, partner organizations, and key stakeholders. Sharing the vision, mission, and goals was easy. The hard part would be implementation, because that required changing the way the department operated for many years. Frank knew this was not going to be easy. (See Appendix C for an example of the department's vision, mission, goals, and objectives.)

After he spoke with Nancy in HR, Frank added an additional topic. He wanted everyone from him and below to be essential employees, sometimes called emergency employees. This meant that, during emergencies, FM employees would be required to be at work (if so informed) unless they were on disability or vacation. Again, Frank met with the union representatives and explained the need. Some of the union representatives were against this requirement but, after many discussions, they agreed. The HR office developed a standard "Essential Employee" form and every employee was required to sign. This would be an annual requirement.

Chapter Twenty-Three
Quality Management and Customer Service

Point To Ponder: Provide timely, safe, dependable service

Facility management is a service-oriented function. The facility management department's service mission must be to deliver safe dependable service so that, in turn, users can accomplish their own missions. Effective customer service stems from sensitivity to the concerns of the departments that rely on facility management and from maintaining adequate communication with all concerned participants.

It was Frank's experience that customers expect the facility management department to have these qualities:

- Be dependable and deliver safe, consistent service.
- Be timely and provide responsive service.
- Provide prompt resolution of problems and issues.
- Keep them informed and updated.

Because the department was going through a change management process and implementing a department vision, mission, goals, Frank thought it important to focus his thinking on quality management and customer service. He knew that good customer service was a prerequisite for success. He realized, too, that the department had a long way to go before it met or exceeded customer expectations.

One afternoon Rona walked into Frank's office to deliver some mail. Frank, who had been thinking about how to improve quality and customer service, asked Rona why she thought the department had a tarnished reputation when it came to quality and customer service. After thinking for a minute, Rona replied that what customers perceive is reality. If the FM department doesn't communicate with them very often, or effectively, they will perceive that the department is mediocre and doesn't care.

She noted that the changes being implemented throughout the department would have a positive effect. Employees were already beginning to discuss the changes; some were even looking forward to them. Even the managers were hopeful. But, Rona added, most of the customers didn't see or experience any change.

Frank went home that night and told his wife about his conversation with Rona. She noted that they were already initiating a newsletter for the department. She then suggested that they send copies (electronic and paper) to their customers as well, adding that it would be a great way to let them know what the department was doing as well as the challenges it was facing.

She then echoed Rona's comment that it's not the quality of service the department gives, but the quality of service the customer perceives. After weighing his wife's and Rona's observations, Frank concluded that customer perception was based on what the customers do or do not experience. Sharing information could help shape perception.

At the next morning meeting, Frank raised the issue of quality management and customer service. He asked everyone to provide him their thoughts when they could. Following the meeting, George told Frank about his previous night's MBA class during which they discussed how organizations should seek to continuously improve and then share that information with others.

George added that, somehow, they needed to include this idea of continuous improvement in their plan. Later that afternoon, Frank ran into Paul, who indicated he'd been thinking about the morning's meeting. Paul said that whatever the department did for quality and customer service, it needed to measure what and how it was doing.

Frank reflected on the comments from his wife, Rona, George, and Paul. He decided to hold a brainstorming session Friday afternoon with George, Paul, and Rona, and include Jim and Bill as well. During the session, he used his typical doodling on the whiteboard. As each person made comments, Frank added annotation to the board.

When they finished, they had developed a list of actions focused on improving quality management and customer service:

- Meet and ask customers to define their service needs.
- Develop a plan for continuous improvement.
- Develop Key Performance Indicators for customer service.
- Conduct training on customer service and employee empowerment.
- Develop and implement a marketing plan for customers (internal/external).
- Emphasize employee appearance and keeping the workplace clean.

Frank took these actions home and dedicated time to begin developing a strategy to improve quality and service provided customers. He thought these actions could be linked to the department's objectives supporting the goals of improving the quality of customer service and customer satisfaction. Then, at Monday morning's meeting, he distributed copies of his proposed strategy to each manager and supervisor. Essentially, it was Frank's effort to develop a facility management marketing plan. Frank thought this was extremely important, especially for the senior leadership.

1. Meet with customers, perhaps on a quarterly basis, to address their concerns about the service provided, inform them of the upcoming changes, and explain how the customers can assist in better planning to reduce downtime and improve service.
2. Make use of signs and slogans that focus on the FM business through the eyes of the customers.
3. Set quality service goals as key performance indicators.
4. Motivate employees to take pride in what they do and in their appearance.
5. To facilitate use of the Customer Service Evaluation form, make the form available online at the university website or on the facility department page for the users to complete. The director will review the comment cards. Trained responsible FM personnel will follow up all cards with negative comments.
6. Establish an FM department newsletter with primary focus on employees. Send these newsletters both electronically and by hard copy. Also send the newsletter to major stakeholders in the university.
7. Establish an award and recognition program for employees that is customer service driven. Frank had observed that they can get more

from the behavior that is rewarded, e.g., a designated parking space for the employee of the month.

8. Publish a facilities services pamphlet, both printed and on the website, explaining to all university staff, faculty, and students how work is managed, how work requests are submitted, and how projects should be initiated.
9. Implement a quality management and customer service training program for all employees. The focus of the training is on improving communication, promoting cooperation, and expanding employee knowledge of quality management skills, attitudes, and habits.
10. Develop a YouTube video of what the department does; showcase the employees at work.

After going through this process, Frank felt comfortable the department was on the right track. He asked the managers and supervisors to review and suggest any modifications. He realized it would take time and dedication, but eventually quality management of the department's services to its customers would be realized. He was also thankful and impressed that all the managers wanted this effort to succeed.

Chapter Twenty-Four
Planning and Budgeting

Point To Ponder: Planning is ultimately linked to the budget

Frank is a planner. He learned through many experiences that planning aligns short-term needs with long-term goals. Good planning is a means of avoiding catastrophe and improving management within the organization. After reading *The Facility Management Handbook*, he understood and considered two types of planning: strategic and mid-range. Both types are linked to the FM department's budget through the annual work plan.

The university business plan and master plan were the main drivers of strategic planning within the FM department. Frank realized the need to comprehend the university business plan; he was very much aware how it shaped the FM plan and the department's budgeting. The FM budget was one of the largest within the university and was based on facility programs, which are part of FM plans. Because the budget was so large, it was a constant target to be reduced.

To plan effectively, the FM department needed to have the following information about the facilities and the overall university business plan. This information would enable the FM department to provide a meaningful forecast.

- Facility asset inventory, including condition assessment and life cycle analysis;
- Utilization information of how the facilities are being used;
- Cost of operating the facilities;

- Applicable cost indexes for the local area;
- University planned growth or reduction considerations;
- Design standards;
- Utility cost and trends;
- Master plan information;
- Personnel needs;
- Sustainability plans; and
- Deferred maintenance information.

Strategic or long-range plans look out more than 3 years—usually 3 to 5 years. Frank reflected that the military looks 20 years out. Long-range plans involve capital-type project work. Priorities often change, so these plans should be periodically reviewed. Because long-range plans look so far out, they are very general and not specific.

Mid-range plans are usually 18 months to 3 years out. These plans are more specific than long-range strategic plans, which is why they are also known as tactical plans. Approximately 70% of these plans flow into the FM annual work plan. Mid-range plans are particularly important for the budget process; time must be spent ensuring that their specificity and assumptions are in much greater detail than long-range plans.

Frank's understanding was that once the university business plan had been analyzed, the capital project needs to support that plan would flow into the capital budget. Unlike his annual operation budget, the capital budget is a multiyear budget. The first item to be assessed would be the need for space. Once that was determined, discussion would revolve around whether it was best to lease, build new, or renovate by making more efficient use of existing space.

The financial affairs VP would decide what could and could not be capitalized based on tax law and university rules. Frank knew when preparing a capital budget there were several considerations. First, he would collect the required elements, which would probably be funded based on a funding target provided by the financial affairs office; he would add 20–30 percent to that amount.

Once the requirements were collected, they would be analyzed and rank ordered based on specific, meaningful criteria developed by the organization. The most common criteria include return on investment (ROI), cash payback, net present value (NPV), and benefit-cost ratio (BCR). Next, the university planning team would review the list and prioritize. The final step was to present the list to the university's leadership, which could also reprioritize the list.

Plan formats are not standardized. The format is important to make these plans easier to understand. Planners often use different formats and procedures, which can make presenting, defending, and comprehending more difficult. Occasionally planners modify formats and procedures from plan to plan and year to year, which causes confusion.

Frank had always thought that standardization was the way to go, and he espoused the format below from *The Facility Management Handbook*:

- Introduction. This sets the stage and tone of the plan.
- Environmental. Relevant environmental considerations that affect facilities are included, for example, utility rate trends or local labor rate projections. These considerations are important to help planners and management better understand the facility plan.
- Assumptions. To plan effectively, you have to look into the future and make assumptions accordingly. Things to consider might include in-house vs. outsourcing, or lease vs. build vs. purchase.
- Constraints. These may be related to growth caps. For example, the organization will have zero growth for the next five years. Or, no additional lease space will be allowed for the next three years.
- Discussion. As part of the discussion, include various scenarios such as fiscal, projected, or rational approaches. The main purpose of this section is to present and explain impacts on each program and situation. This section is probably the most important one and requires the FM input.
- Conclusions. Major conclusions that support the organization's business plan are presented.
- Recommendations. The FM recommends the preferable course of action.
- Appendices. Include any information or data that support the recommendations and conclusions.

Approximately 70 percent of the annual work plan (AWP) comes from the mid-range plan. The remaining 30 percent of the annual plan's requirements must still be collected and integrated into the plan. These include operations and maintenance expenses to support daily functions along with any revenues and chargebacks. This 30 percent also includes salaries, benefits, insurance, office supplies, mail, postage, telecommunications, automation, clothing and uniforms, and utilities.

The AWP is specific and detailed, meaning a working cost estimate has been prepared. The AWP should also be easily updated and maintained. Frank planned to initiate a Program Budget Advisory Committee (PBAC) as a means to prioritize and align the AWP requirements with the capital plan. Members of the PBAC would include Frank's direct report managers. He also planned to invite other department heads to participate because of their knowledge and expertise.

According to Frank, the AWP should be consistent and trackable from year to year. The FM programs found in the annual work plan are linked to the FM budget. Unlike capital budgets, operating budgets are normally prepared for one year, based on the calendar or fiscal year. However, Frank knew that the FM department was likely involved with three budgets in any fiscal year: the current year closeout budget, execution of the current budget, and developing the next FY budget.

At the same time, the department would be involved with two AWPs: current year execution and the one being prepared for next year. Frank's experience was that one of two things happen with the annual work plan. Either the work plan was developed after the budget is approved or, during the budget development, the work plan was not updated. As a result, there could be a big difference between the approved budget and the approved work plan. Hence, it was essential to carefully manage the planning and budgeting processes.

What did Frank identify as the characteristics of the FM operating budget? His experience indicated he was responsible to quantify and justify growth in the FM budget and to structure the budget based on the way the department operated. He noticed there was no procedure established to identify work that had to be done. He thought of it as *impromptu* planning, which he was not used to. Some of the requirements and procedures he had already implemented would help to better identify the work and improve planning.

To build a budget, an FM director has to know all the items to be included in the budget. This requires thorough knowledge of the budget cycle. In the case of the university the budget year started on July 1.

Therefore, the following cycle had to be followed:

- July–August: Gather information (planned renovations, service contracts, etc.)
- September–October: Budget guidance issued
- November–December: Budget draft submission
- January–March: Budget discussions
- April–May: Budget finalized
- July 1: Budget implemented

The AWP drives the annual budget. For discretionary annual projects, Frank has always planned 15 percent over the budget guidance because some projects drop out during the year. These additional projects (the 15 percent) should be ready to substitute if planned projects drop out. When completed for submission, the budget details total cost, provides comparative costs (e.g., cost from previous year), and uses standard unit costs. Individual subunit manager responsibilities are identified so they can be held accountable.

Before submitting the final department budget, Frank planned to conduct several analyses. These would include historical comparisons (e.g., previous years to the present), unit cost comparison to determine if there was a change in the unit cost—and, if so, why—and, finally, a trend analysis. He then planned to make variances a principal part of the budget narrative. In addition, new issues would be discussed. Frank used the Facility Manager's Guide to Finance and Budgeting to help him develop the analyses.

If funding guidance turned out to be lower than the stated requirements, then a description of the impact caused by the constraints would be developed, by category. Frank looked at the budget as a tool that explained the cost of doing business and what would happen if funding were not made available. Based on what he learned to date, he knew he had to become intimately familiar with how to develop the budget, manage it, and defend it.

Chapter Twenty-five
Fire Protection

Point To Ponder: Develop and implement fire protection inspections and protocols

Frank was doing his daily MBWA on the campus when he walked into the parking garage. He had walked through this garage dozens of times in the last few months, but today something caught his attention. He looked up and saw the dry pipe sprinkler system pipe and noticed rubber clamps. As he walked along observing the pipe, he counted at least 20 rubber clamps and he could see many more. He thought to himself, "This is odd. Why so many clamps?"

When he got back to his office, he decided to speak with Paul Larson, the central shops manager. He found Paul in the hallway near one of the shops and explained what he saw. Paul did not know the answer but suggested they go to the plumbing shop and ask. There they found Chuck Martin, the plumbing foreman. Chuck was a crusty older man; Frank thought probably in his late 60s. He had started in the shop 30 years ago as a helper. He then took courses and applied for his licenses through the years and achieved his journeyman and master plumber's licenses and then his gasfitter's license. He knew the details of every plumbing system in every building. It was all in his head.

Frank was impressed listening to Chuck. When Frank described what he had seen, Chuck immediately explained that when the contractor installed the sprinkler pipe, he submitted a change order to install Schedule 10 black iron pipe in lieu of Schedule 40 black iron pipe. This was supposed to be a cost-savings measure. The design engineer approved the change and the contractor installed the pipe. A year earlier, the construction inspector positions had been abolished because of budget deficits. The thinking was that the shops could keep an eye on contract work installations.

Chuck told Frank that no one would listen that depending on the shop tradesmen to check and inspect contract work was a nonstarter. The tradesmen just don't have the time to watch contractors. As a result, the pipe was installed with inadequate pitch and it had several slight sags. Chuck then described how condensation builds up in the pipe over time. Every year the plumbers drained the pipe at the drip legs in preparation for cold weather, but not all the water could be drained. Thus, there was condensation buildup, and oxygen entering the pipe from testing and draining eventually caused corrosion.

Because Schedule 10 iron pipe was thinner than Schedule 40, pinhole leaks began to appear faster. When the small leaks were spotted, the plumbers installed clamps. Chuck summarized that those clamps were what Frank saw in the garage. Anticipating Frank's question about why they didn't replace the pipe, Chuck noted the answer was cost. It would have cost approximately $250,000 to replace the sprinkler pipe in that garage. The department did not have that amount of money available because the deferred maintenance was in the millions.

Both Frank and Paul were impressed with Chuck's knowledge. Three issues filtered through Frank's mind immediately. First, for future presentations concerning the budget and staffing shortages, he needed to document what Chuck had just explained. He could use that information as an example of cutting off your nose to spite your face, and the ultimate cost in money and potential safety issues. Second, Frank had heard that National Fire Protection Association (NFPA) Standard 13-2019 had a requirement for water supply corrosion monitoring.

He asked Paul to research the NFPA and verify that information. Frank was thinking he could also use that information to make the case to replace the sprinkler pipe and to point out the need for inspectors. Third, Chuck had a great amount of knowledge in his head, but it needed to be documented. Frank considered temporarily removing Chuck from the plumbing shop for a few months and instead have him go through building plans in the archives to update the "as-built" drawings. Frank decided he would discuss this with Paul.

As the three men walked toward the outside entrance, Frank saw a fire hydrant on the sidewalk adjacent to the shop door. The hydrant reminded him to ask Chuck one more question. He told Chuck that he'd received a call the day before from a city fire department lieutenant who'd wanted to meet with Frank that afternoon to discuss hydrants. Frank asked Chuck if he could attend the impromptu meeting; he asked Paul as well.

When the fire department lieutenant arrived, Frank introduced him to Paul and Chuck. The lieutenant explained that the city's Fire Chief appointed him to lead a special group to inspect all fire hydrants in the city. The intent was to standardize them. The lieutenant explained that the hose connection threads on hydrants were not standard size. This could be problem when a fire truck arrived at the scene of a fire and tried to connect the pumper truck to the hydrant but didn't have the correct coupling.

Therefore, the chief wanted all the hydrants inspected and standardized. The lieutenant stated that he decided to start inspecting the hydrants at the university the following week. Frank asked Chuck how many hydrants there were on campus; Chuck responded there are 32. Frank then offered the lieutenant any assistance he needed and designated Chuck as the point of contact.

The next week the fire department team arrived and began inspecting all 32 hydrants. After one week of inspections and flow testing, using a pitot tube, the lieutenant met again with Frank and Chuck to brief them on the results. Of the 32 hydrants inspected, 14 had treads that were different and two hydrants had flow problems; these would need to be replaced. Frank thanked the lieutenant for the inspections and the briefing and indicated they would follow up and keep him updated.

After the lieutenant departed, Frank asked Chuck to get prices to replace the 16 hydrants. This was one more expense for which Frank would have to find funding. If the hydrants were not replaced, the city would fine the university. The fine was one thing, but the reputation of the university would be tarnished once the news media broke the story.

Frank also told Chuck to ensure the tops of the hydrants are painted in accordance with the National Fire Protection Association (NFPA) 291 guideline. Chuck asked why. Frank explained the colors indicate the flow capacity of the hydrant, so firefighters know the hydrant's water pumping capacity when they connect the pumper truck to the hydrant. For example: Red indicates a water flow capacity of 500 gallons per minute (GPM); orange 500-999 GPM; green 1,000-1499 GPM; blue 1,500 GPM or greater. Additionally, Frank told Chuck that a hydrant painted all yellow indicates it is connected to the public water supply system; whereas a hydrant painted all violet is fed from a lake or pond.

Next, Frank decided to meet with Paul to discuss fire protection and prevention. The electrical shop oversaw the functioning and operation of the fire protection systems throughout the university. The foreman of the electrical shop, Craig Johnson, also managed a fire protection contract with a local fire protection company. Frank explained to Craig and Paul his concern about fire impairment.

Years earlier, he had experienced a technician shutting off the fire protection sprinkler system while working on it. When finished, the technician forgot to turn the system back on and went home. That night the fire alarm was activated when a coffee urn overheated and caught fire. Several occupants were overcome by smoke and were hospitalized. The risk insurer refused to pay for damages because a "fire impairment form" was not called in. If an impairment had been submitted, the risk insurer would have followed up at the end of the workday and asked if the work was completed and if a fire watch was initiated.

Frank also wanted to know if the department fire plan included internal protocols to contact the Authority Having Jurisdiction (AHJ); how FM employees responded to fire alarms; training needs and protective equipment use; fire impairment procedures; facility intelligence (which included location of fire protection control valves, fire pump locations, and operations); and fire detection and suppression systems. Craig responded that they had some of that information, but it was not assembled into one document. He added that they just needed time to collect more information and organize it.

Frank tried to maintain his composure as he thought about Craig's explanation. He emphasized to Paul that this was a life safety issue that could not be put on the back burner. It had to be made a top priority. He instructed Paul, if necessary, to break Craig away for a few weeks and have him research and compile the fire plan information. Frank wanted to be kept updated, but made it clear he expected to see in a short timeframe a completed fire plan that had been coordinated with the AHJ. He added that, if Paul had questions or needed his assistance, Paul could always see him. In concluding, he instructed Paul to give him periodic updates at the 8:00 A.M. morning meetings.

Chapter Twenty-six
Indoor Air Quality

Point To Ponder: Follow your established indoor air quality protocols and checklists

The dean of the Business and Management School was holding a department meeting with ten faculty members and his executive assistant. The conference room where the meeting was held was an interior space with no windows, a large conference room table, and chairs for 12 people. After the first 30 minutes, all the attendees were getting sleepy and starting to doze off—partly because the topic was boring to them, but also because the room was stuffy and held the maximum number of people for its size. Everyone was trying to pay attention, but the warm room was overtaking them.

The dean, realizing the meeting was not accomplishing any of the goals he had set, decided to end the meeting and stood up. The attendees immediately stood and, when the door was opened, they all felt better because of the gush of cooler air that rushed into the room. The dean realized the room should have better ventilation. He directed his executive assistant to call a work request to the facilities department.

The executive assistant went online and submitted the work request. The work management center (WMC)—sometimes called the call center—received the work request along with the other 150 or so it received every day. The WMC supervisor then reviewed each work request. In this case, the supervisor decided this work request from the dean would be considered an indoor air quality issue (IAQ). All IAQ work requests were sent to the FM director at his request.

Frank had experienced numerous IAQ issues throughout his career. One example he recalled occurred in an office building where the occupants complained of sewer smell. These occupants had only recently moved into this vacant space. Frank and his plumbing foreman went to look for themselves. They diagnosed the problem as a floor drain in a common area of the building; the drain had dried out. This particular common area had been vacant for several months and no custodial cleaning had occurred. When custodians mopped the floor, water would fill the trap and contain the sewer gas. Because the space had been vacant for so long, the trap had dried out. Frank's plumbing foreman said he would fill the trap with mineral oil. That would contain the gas and it would not evaporate the way water does.

Indoor Air Quality is a major problem which must be resolved. Frank decided years earlier that he would review every IAQ case. He had educated himself on indoor air quality. He knew about the causes, how to minimize them, the need for inspections, system maintenance, good custodial services, source management, and the need for an established policy. Frank also understood that indoor air quality could become an emergency if building systems, operations and maintenance, and construction/renovation were operated or performed arbitrarily without any thought of the impact to building occupants.

Throughout his career, Frank had built a strong reputation as a manager who followed up and could be trusted to accomplish the mission. He had developed credibility not only with his staff but also with his peers and the organization's leadership. In every IAQ situation, he publicized the IAQ situation that was being examined in department newsletters.

He discussed them in working lunches and sent personal emails to key people within the organization and to building occupants. He wanted everyone to know that the facilities management department took IAQ situations seriously and would provide as healthy an indoor work environment as possible. He knew that good communications were important to significantly reduce the possibility that this topic could develop into a media nightmare and, ultimately, into a crisis.

Looking at the submitted work request, Frank thought he knew what the problem was. But he had been down this road before and learned that sometimes assumptions were not always correct. His experience told him to take each complaint seriously; to do otherwise would invite worse trouble. Years earlier, Frank had written a department policy and procedure for indoor air quality. The policy and the procedure spelled out what needed to be done in what sequence.

Frank decided he would appoint a manager to investigate this specific IAQ complaint. He knew it was good management to have one principal manager examine the complaint, keep information confidential, and handle the follow up in an appropriate manner. For this case, he appointed his deputy George, who had training in mechanical systems and had previous IAQ experience.

George developed his protocol to tackle the IAQ issue at the business school's conference room. He first inspected and analyzed building mechanical systems, building operations, and test data. Because the conference room was internal, George decided to start his inspection by checking the computer data base for any previous work requests for this room. He looked for trends but found none.

George then reviewed the building's technical data: air-handling system mechanical drawings, building specification documents, test and balance reports, and maintenance data. He analyzed this information to understand and evaluate the operation of the building and its mechanical systems. He then conducted a visual inspection of the heating, ventilation, and air conditioning (HVAC) systems. He looked at coils, condensate drainage, fan chambers, humidifiers, controlling hardware, and state of filters. He had airborne microbial samples taken to determine bacterial and fungal species present.

Finally, he had instrument tests conducted at various locations throughout the building and specifically the conference room. He measured carbon dioxide and carbon monoxide levels of the empty room at 800 PPM (parts per million). He knew that carbon dioxide levels rise rapidly in poorly ventilated space because exhaled air is about 4 percent carbon dioxide by volume. As it turned out, another meeting was scheduled to start; George asked if he could sit in to measure the air quality. As people came into the room, the readings started rising and showed a carbon dioxide level of 1,000 PPM (parts per million), the threshold at which a room begins to feel stuffy, according to the American Society of Heating, Refrigeration, and Air-Conditioning Engineers (ASHRAE). After 30 minutes, the readings spiked at 1,700 PPM.

George knew that buildings should operate with sufficient outside air. The amount of outside air used should follow ASHRAE Standard 62.1. By introducing a sufficient volume of outside air, two benefits will accrue. First, indoor air pollutants will be sufficiently reduced so as not to annoy building occupants.

Second, by routinely introducing more outside air into the building than is exhausted, the building is placed in positive pressure. This will preclude a natural inflow of unfiltered air through the building.

In this specific case, George knew that lowering the temperature for that space when it was occupied would automatically increase the relative humidity and lessen occupant sensitivity. He also knew that people perceive cooler air to be cleaner and fresher. George also checked the supply air diffusers to verify they were not covered. He found none of them covered. He decided to check the supply air diffusers in every space on that floor.

Occupants of space often cover diffusers if conditioned air is blowing on them. While these actions are understandable, they result in the occupied spaces being denied the proper amount of outside air. Covering the supply air diffusers, in turn, impacts the proper air balance in that space. This results in some areas receiving too much supply air, while others receive too little.

George's inspection found covered diffusers. He knew he had some options and discussed them with Frank. One option was to recommend that occupant locations, where the diffusers were covered, be relocated. A second option was to change the diffuser design. Frank asked his deputy to discuss the options with the dean of the business school. The dean did not want to relocate people because they were already restricted and strapped for space. So, George made notes to modify the diffuser design.

George next checked the maintenance of the air handling systems. He looked at the preventive maintenance (PM) plan. He noted that the schedules, tasks, and procedures were accomplished on a timely basis. He considered that many PM plans failed because the schedules were not followed, but this was not the case here.

Continuing his inspection, he checked custodial services. He checked the cleaning plan, then spoke with the supervisor and a few custodians. He learned that cleaning tasks—including vacuuming, buffing, and sweeping—were completed during the off hours, between 10 P.M. and 7 A.M. He was surprised to see portable high-efficiency particulate air (HEPA) vacuums were used. He noted that the cleaning products used contained no volatile organic compounds (VOC).

Following the department policy and protocol he developed for this IAQ issue, George examined possible sources of pollutants. He looked at office equipment that could give off noxious gas in the form of VOC chemicals and particulates. He reviewed whether the area had been recently renovated and considered the feasibility of installing a separate dedicated exhaust system. Once he had completed this review, he went to the final step: the final report.

George used the checklists the FM department had developed through experience with IAQ issues. He decided to include these checklists as appendixes to the final report. He started with the initial IAQ Incident and Complaint logs. When he interviewed various people in the business school, he used the IAQ Interview log. He included the IAQ HVAC Management checklist and the IAQ Management checklist. He summarized the complaint and inspection results and included his findings and recommendations.

Once completed, he delivered the report to Frank; he knew Frank would want to discuss his findings. George's conclusion was the operations, maintenance, custodial services, and source management were being conducted as they should. George said he would follow-up on the diffuser design change and increase the amount of outside air.

Once they agreed on the report, Frank delivered it to the department dean to discuss and implement George's recommendations. The dean was gratified with the speed and thoroughness of the investigation and complimented George. As Frank departed the dean's office, he reflected that he had made an ally who would favorably support facilities management in the future.

Chapter Twenty-seven
Workplace Violence

Point To Ponder: Ensure adequate workplace safety and security measures are in place

It was a cool, balmy day. Frank was in his office reviewing paperwork and sending emails to clients. Frank was a busy administrator, who managed a department now consisting of 275 employees, downsized from 350 employees. Among the technicians, custodians, administrative assistants, clerks, and subordinate supervisors and managers in his department, Frank had 12 managers who reported directly to him.

Frank knew the preferred number of direct reports was three to five. However, because of the downsizing, the managerial structure was flattened. Frank did not like having so many direct reports because he could not spend enough time with each one. Although he was organized, he had papers and textbooks scattered on his conference table and desk. The shelves behind his desk were crammed with various studies of building systems, policies, and operating procedures.

Late last week, one of Frank's subordinate managers gave one of his employee's progressive discipline. The employee—a heating, ventilation, and air conditioning technician (HVAC)—had an attendance problem. For the previous two months, the employee had called in sick on Monday or Friday. After three times calling in sick, the employee was given verbal counseling. The next time it occurred, the employee was given written counseling and told that, if this behavior continued, it would result in more severe discipline.

A few weeks went by and the employee called in sick, again. He even provided a doctor's statement for being sick. The manager read the statement and reviewed the individual's time and attendance record. The manager decided that since this was the fourth time within six weeks that the employee called in sick, and the employee had received a verbal and written counselling, he would issue a progressive disciplinary warning. The warning was given the next day. The employee was not happy.

When the manager asked the employee why he called in sick on those days, the employee stated it was none of the manager's business. A few days later, as the manager toured a building, he spoke with several cleaning employees. The manager liked to walk one of his buildings every day. He enjoyed management by walking around (MBWA) because he could speak with employees. MBWA gave him an opportunity to learn what was really happening within the work force.

He knew he could find out more about employee feelings and issues by simply asking questions one-on-one. He had taken a course in communications and knew this process was called the "informal network." He collected much of his information this way. The manager had learned this from Frank, who had been his mentor. Frank often gave the manager tips and discussed the importance of policies and procedures as well as the need for being prepared. The manager was a good student!

The cleaning employees knew about the progressive discipline issued to the HVAC technician. The situation had been discussed by many of the department's employees, all of whom were waiting to see what would happen. The manager asked the cleaning employees if they knew about the situation, which they did. As the manager continued to ask questions, he learned some things of which he had been unaware. Apparently, the HVAC technician had a small company that performed HVAC residential maintenance and installations at night and weekends, and on his vacation days. This was the reason the technician would call in sick on Monday or Friday.

The manager had followed the organization policy, which stated that verbal and written counselling had to be given before more severe discipline could be issued. Employees had received a training class on all the organization policies and operating procedures. Managers and supervisors had received the same training. The manager decided to have a private conversation with the HVAC technician to explain the next step in the disciplinary progression.

He did not want the technician terminated because he was a good technician, but the policy had to be followed. The manager knew that Frank was keeping an eye on this issue; if the manager did not follow the policy, he would be disciplined. In addition, the technician knew the strain the manager was under, but he had a small company and had to continue to satisfy his customers.

A few weeks later, the technician again called in sick on Monday. He had a residential HVAC installation over the weekend but ran into a technical issue and needed parts. Because the supply house was closed on Sunday, he had to wait until they opened on Monday morning. He made the decision to call in sick one more time.

On Tuesday, the manager decided to continue the progressive discipline. The next step was termination. The manager had the paperwork typed and called the technician to his office. He summarized the technician's attendance record, briefly reviewed the policy, and finally issued the termination letter. The HVAC technician was angry. He needed the job because of the benefits it provided for his family. He made threats to the manager and against Frank that he would "get even."

The manager collected the technician's identification card, keys and key card, and radio. He told the technician that he was not to come to this area in the future. If he had business with the organization, he was to check in with the security office. He then had another employee accompany the technician to his locker where he could clean it out. The informal employee network buzzed; all the employees were watching to see what would happen.

Following the termination, the manager briefed Frank on the episode. Frank recommended the manager also brief the security office on what took place and give them information about the technician. Both men, however, dismissed the threats as insignificant.

Two weeks later, an employee who was very dependable and informative stopped by Frank's office. Frank had an open-door policy. His employees knew they could go by his office anytime he was not busy and speak with him. This employee told Frank he saw the HVAC technician the day before in the lobby of the building. The employee was speaking with other department employees, stating he planned to get even with Frank and the manager for terminating him. Learning this, Frank became concerned for the safety of the manager and the people in the building.

Frank decided to inform the security office that the HVAC technician had been seen in the building a day earlier. He informed the organization leadership of what had happened and actions taken. As a proactive measure, he informed the local police about what had taken place. Frank discussed with the organization's legal office as to whether a restraining order could be issued. He also informed the vice president of human resources. He realized some of his employees may be concerned and upset of the possibility of a workplace violence issue, and they may want or need counseling.

According to *The Report to the Nation on Workplace Violence*, there are four categories of workplace violence: criminal intent, customer/client violence, worker on worker, and personal relationships. Frank realized that, if the former employee committed a violent act, it would be considered a type III category (worker on worker) workplace violence incident. He determined that additional training for the entire department was needed. The focus should be on what constitutes workplace violence, with specific emphasis on the policies and procedures and how to handle such an incident.

Frank knew that, once informed or knowledgeable of a violent situation, an employer is liable for the action of its employees if adequate safety and security measures are not taken. He also initiated a physical safety and security survey to determine areas of concern related to workplace violence. Frank then implemented a series of protection and prevention actions he had learned in one of the textbooks crammed onto his shelf.

As he thought about the emotional impact a violent incident can have on employees, Frank recognized that recovery can be a major process. Frank decided that if something happened it would be important for him to be visible to employees. He knew from years of experience, especially MBWA, employees would want to talk and ask questions. They might also require counselling.

Chapter Twenty-eight
Annual Report

Point To Ponder: Tell the FM story to all stakeholders

Frank knew the university aspired to be world class and he wanted his facility management department to be considered world class as well. He thought summarizing the department's activities into an annual report would help facility managers at other universities succeed; in turn, perhaps they would share their experience with him and his department, thereby assisting with benchmarking.

As a bonus, he thought the annual report could be a good marketing tool. Frank wanted to tell the FM story. He believed he knew his audience and how the leadership of the university thought. He wanted to provide a clear picture of what facility management does for them.

An annual report would enable Frank to share his experiences, both successes and failures, and the knowledge he and the department had amassed. He believed in himself, that he knew what he was doing. But he also wanted the university's leadership and employees to believe in him, thereby cementing both his and the department's credibility.

Frank knew that annual reports vary in format: graphs, charts, and narrative. For this first report, he had several goals:

- Summarize what his department had achieved this past year, changes being made, and what they learned;
- Inform the leadership of issues that needed to be addressed;

- Talk about the many heroes in the department and the challenges they faced;
- Expound on the importance and critical need for technology, especially as the university expands;
- Include positive stories from customers about how FM employees assisted them;
- Promote the value his employees provided the university;
- Describe some of the challenges the FM department faced; and
- Explain the challenges that still needed to be addressed.

Frank knew this first annual report would be significant as a marketing tool. Therefore, it had to appeal and capture the interest of all who read it. Because he wanted it to be sophisticated in design and layout, Frank asked a good friend who had marketing experience to help him.

First, Frank decided to recap the newsletters developed by Rona during the first year. The second and third parts of the report would summarize what he and the other managers worked on. He developed a template to follow, asking each manager to list items that should be included. Frank knew this approach would not be all encompassing, but it was a start. If he could succeed with an enticing layout and design, he thought there was a chance to appeal to the readers. He also decided to provide both hard copy print and electronic versions.

Part I:
- Summary of the newsletters, including lots of photos of employees
- Listing of new employees and departing employees

Part II:
- Summary of each shop
- Any specific issues that impacted the university and what was done to ameliorate
- Developed vision, mission, goals, and values

Part III:
- Summary of actions completed and in progress
- The number of work orders received and completed
- Charts depicting equipment replacement, costs, and expenses

Frank projected that the following year's annual report would focus on achieving the department's mission, vision, goals, challenges, accomplishments, and financial data. He would ensure there were graphics that showed trends resulting from the metrics the department tracked.

Specific areas for that report would include:

- Service order summary
- Energy usage
- Preventive maintenance
- Space utilization
- O&M project summary
- Sustainability
- Budget summary
- Emergencies
- Capital project summary
- Summary of key performance indicators

Chapter Twenty-nine
Change with the Times

Point To Ponder: Be open-minded and emphasize communication

Toward the end of his first year on the job, Frank spent time reminiscing about his life and how he eventually became a facility manager. He had not ever contemplated such a career. In each situation and position he held, he gained knowledge which carried over to a new position. He remembered the adage, *"The older you get, the wiser you become,"* and thought how true this was. As we grow older, we gain a better perspective of our surroundings and what we have learned through our experiences.

In every facility management or public works position he held throughout his career, Frank experienced reactive responses to operations and maintenance because of budget restrictions. Reacting to situations was akin to managing emergencies, which led to his motto, *"We have to be prepared for anything; we're in the emergency response business."*

But times continued to change. Technology enabled the department to manage and conduct business faster and better than years earlier. Frank thought about that for some time and concluded it was critical to change with the times.

Facility management is constantly evolving. Rapid advancements in technology have had a sizable impact in how we manage facilities. Older employees are retiring. Their legacy knowledge must somehow be captured. Younger employees are looking for challenges with companies that welcome open-mindedness and allow them to speak their minds. As a re-

sult, organizational culture is coming to the forefront because FM leaders have a workforce made up of various generations: baby boomers, Generation X, Millennials, and Generation Z. They all think differently.

Taking these changes into account, Frank thought about how important it was for all managers and supervisors to understand and appreciate each generation's work styles and beliefs. For example, baby boomers (1946–1964) want to get the job done, spending whatever time and effort necessary to do that. For them work is the first priority. Generation X (1965–1980) also want to get the job done, but believe rules and policies are flexible. They want a balanced family and work life.

Millennials (1981–1996) don't follow schedules and work to deadlines. They blend work and their personal lives together. Generation Z (1996–present) are well-educated and dependent on technology. They resemble Millennials in many ways but are more racially and ethnically diverse. They want job flexibility and ethical leadership.

Frank realized that understanding the four generations and how they work together would be critical to job success and quality service. He then focused on hiring and training, realizing that hiring practices for new employees need to be altered. Frank learned managers and foremen interviewed job candidates by themselves and that candidates were often selected based on friendships or family ties as opposed to qualification and suitability for the position.

Frank was determined to change that practice. He stated that going forward he wanted a panel of 3 to 5 people, with at least one woman on the panel. George countered, asking why they needed a woman on the interview panel given that they have no technical experience. Frank told George he was incorrect, noting that women frequently attend technical trade schools and were just as qualified as men.

Furthermore, he theorized that women frequently look at applicants as to whether their personalities would fit in with the organization culture, values, and operational methods. By contrast, men were often more focused on whether the applicant could do the job.

Frank then offered another example from a previous position where they needed to fill a vacancy in the solid waste and recycling section. When a female applied and was interviewed, Frank had first been skeptical, but decided to take the risk and hire her. She would be the only woman in the crew of 20 men. The work was dirty and physically taxing. The men did not care about their appearance; they were unshaven, scruffy, disheveled, and used foul language.

Once this woman joined the section, the crew cleaned up both themselves and the shop. Her presence had a major positive impact on the functioning of this section. Frank added that, despite her size, she more than kept up with the work.

Frank reasserted that training was essential to how the department functioned. They needed to train all managers, supervisors, and employees on how to communicate with each other while respecting their differences. He hoped this would result in greater tolerance of generational differences, cultivating an attitude for teamwork and respect, and resulting in greater customer service.

He then noted the facility management profession was going through transformation, driven by innovative technology. Frank's experience was that trade employees would no longer be promoted into the facility management leadership positions simply because it was their time. Instead, today's facility managers must be qualified by way of education and experience. Training and certifications were now more important than ever before and they had to invest in a high-performance workforce if they were going to be successful.

Frank anticipated that changes in future facility management operations and maintenance would be driven by innovation and technology. Artificial intelligence (AI) would play a major role. He constantly told his managers that all of them needed to be knowledgeable of technology, staying current with advances, and how technology could better serve the department.

Technological changes would drive productivity, quality management and customer service, partnering, sustainability, and energy management. Productivity would increase because employees would work smarter and more efficiently. An FM app would help trade employees capture vital information simply and easily. This information, in turn, would help make O&M teams more efficient. The bottom line was that technology would save time.

Frank detailed for his team his views on how technology will impact their work going forward:

- Technology ultimately increases productivity by decreasing the time spent on clerical tasks, such as completing cumbersome paper reports, while capturing data immediately in a central database.
- Increases in efficiency and productivity will also be attributable to

automation. The Internet of Things (IoT) connects smart sensors with objects that utilize technology in order to communicate with devices in a building. These devices can monitor energy usage, then formulate a strategy to save energy and reduce utility costs while also improving building efficiency. These devices can be motion-activated or accessed from smartphones, for example, to control HVAC. In turn, this efficiency will improve the organization's quest for sustainability.

Building automation systems (BAS) are part of the IoT and can improve HVAC in buildings. These systems can notify HVAC technicians when something in the system needs to be checked because it is not operating properly. Ultimately, this information saves time and money while improving service to the customer.

Quality management and customer service will improve because customers/occupants will see that their building is providing them the service they want. This will occur because FM employees have been trained to understand what customers want and how their space is used. Using the IoT to connect the sensors to the building devices will drive efficiency. Restrooms will be equipped with touch-free products, making them safer from infectious disease for occupant use. Artificial intelligence (AI) will be able to analyze building data, identify trends, and offer technicians insights on working more efficiently. Ultimately, energy costs will be reduced and building occupants will be happier—and so will be the facility manager.

Building information modeling (BIM) is a tool that has been used by designers for more than a decade. The O&M aspect of BIM will provide FM departments and technicians the ability to examine their various systems in three dimensions. When integrated with FM software, technicians will be able to retrieve three-dimensional floor plans, asset information, O&M manuals, and warranty information. This integrated visual modelling ability will help make diagnosing equipment problems easier, improve response times, and save costs.

Security will make more and better use of technology. Sensors, actuators, and devices will continue to evolve. Use of drones (unmanned aerial vehicles) could be used for surveillance in unique situations. In addition, drones can also be used to inspect difficult-to-reach areas on buildings; deliver supplies, materials, and tools; look for damage after a storm; and, with mounted infrared cameras, check for roof water saturation. A major consideration when planning to use drones is "follow the existing federal and local laws." FMs need to understand that drones also have a negative aspect because people can use them for their own sinister reasons.

Partnerships with outsourced vendors and contractors will increase. Many of these companies are specialized. By contrast, the FM department is more focused on O&M and does not have the specialized tools, expertise, training, or equipment on hand. It's much easier and cheaper to contract with a company that specializes in specific functions—especially if the arrangement is for several years. Frank thought about his experience with elevator, custodial cleaning, HVAC water treatment, and fire protection contractors. He had implemented contracts with the same companies for upwards of ten years with only slight increases in the contract cost. This longevity essentially cultivated relationships and made these companies part of his organization, resulting in improved service and reduced costs.

The concept of sustainability will expand as resources are reduced and energy costs rise. This will inevitably lead to improved and more efficient use of solar technology. Solid waste management and recycling will increase as technologies are developed to find new uses for materials considered detrimental to the environment. Composting will also expand as new techniques develop. FMs may be asked to help colleges and public works implement composting locations having community gardens. With increased focus on global warming, composting will be advantageous in removing carbon from the air. It will also enrich soil and reduce the need for chemical fertilizers.

Robotic grass mowers will become prevalent. These mowers can operate 7/24, if needed. One technician can operate and manage multiple mowers. These mowers will free up manpower traditionally needed for grounds grass cutting, enabling these workers to learn new skills and contribute to the department in other ways. Robotic floor scrubbers operate in a similar manner. They can clean floors in a building faster than walk-behind auto-scrubbers and hand mopping. Thus, custodians can do other cleaning while the robotic scrubbers clean floors.

Lighting will continue to improve. Lighting involves energy usage, which affects the environment. Energy-efficient lighting uses less electricity and, in turn, a reduction in power plant air-polluting emissions. That impact can significantly influence energy efficiency in existing buildings and spill over to building operations involving water, waste, and overall environmental quality.

The use of electric vehicles will dramatically increase. Demand for carbon fuel (gasoline) will decrease but more electric vehicle charging stations will be needed. These charging stations can be powered by clean fuel such as solar panels.

In some cases, FM shops will use 3D printing to fabricate their own equipment repair parts. These printers could especially be helpful to FMs in emergency situations. Even parts manufacturers will use 3D printing. It may not be economical for FM departments to focus on mass production of 3D printed parts, but in crises situations, it's nice to have a backup.

Changing with the times requires flexibility and adaptability. Frank thought anyone thinking of a career in FM would need to have an open mind to change, develop and maintain a positive caring attitude; be a communicator; have knowledge of business skills; and be technically competent. FM leaders would have to continuously seek to improve and focus on empowering employees to be the best they could be. This would not be easy and would require patience and commitment.

Chapter Thirty
First Year Update

Point To Ponder: Continue keeping the "boss' informed

Frank continued sending updates to his boss. He and his managers had accomplished much in the last twelve months, and he wanted to explain the progress and results. Frank had received positive comments from various faculty and staff members. Many had sent Frank notes and left voicemails supporting the changes the department was implementing. Even students were commenting to facility employees their approval and satisfaction with the changes.

So, Frank summarized ongoing initiatives, issues, and responsibilities. One of the final actions Frank proposed to his boss was to conduct an audit of the department using an outside consultant. The audit would then become the basis to measure improvement and change in the future. This audit would help to show change and improvements when the department was scrutinized in the future for its support of the customer.

Frank's list of actions taken in the first year are below:

- Developed a strategy for moving the department forward. (Frank)
- Developed, with managers and employees, the department vision, mission, goals, and objectives. (Frank, managers, employees)
- Developed the Plan for Change. It included changing work hours to improve support to the university. (Frank, George)
- Implemented requirement that all FM department employees would be considered essential/emergency employees. (Frank, managers,

Nancy)

- Improved communications with employees, staff, and faculty to keep them apprised of the changes and potential impacts. (Frank, managers)
- Implemented the Facility Management Stakeholder Service Council (FMSSC). (Frank)
- Focused on improving quality management and customer service by developing a list of actions which are the prelude of the FM marketing plan. (Frank, managers)
- Reviewed the university business plan and long-range capital plan. Updated the department mid-range O&M plan. Developed the department's first annual work plan, which feeds into the budget. (Frank, managers)
- Reviewed the fire protection systems. Uncovered sprinkler pipe, fire hydrant, and fire impairment issues. (Frank, Chuck plumbing foreman)
- Reviewed IAQ complaint, checklists, and inspection results. Concluded O&M, custodial services, and source management were conducted properly. (Frank, George)
- Initiated a physical safety and security survey to determine areas of concern related to workplace violence. (Frank)
- Developed and implemented the first department annual report. (Frank)
- Planned and initiated a department audit. This audit will focus on events of the first year and set the stage for the next 5–10 years. (Frank)

Chapter Thirty-one
The Final Chapter

Point To Ponder: How to be successful

Finally, Frank thought about the issues and challenges he faced during this first year on the job. For the most part, these were issues and challenges that most FMs will continue to face in the future. He thought of individuals wanting to make facility management their profession, or advance themselves within the profession, and what they would need to be successful.

Several employees, managers, and supervisors had asked him what they can do to advance themselves and make themselves more competitive. At this point in his life, Frank had almost 25 years of experience leading and managing facility and public works departments; he believed he knew what he was doing. So, he decided to list and share the key points that he had learned—sometimes the hard way—throughout his career.

He narrowed the points down to ten. Although they would appear to be simple, they would in fact require practice and training. They would need to become habits, requiring the consistent repetition needed to change behavior. Here is what Frank shared with those who asked for guidance.

First, have a good understanding of financial management. Understand the need for planning, the types of planning, and how planning ultimately feeds into the budget. Know the budget process and remain continuously involved. As Frank often told the managers, "Money drives the train. We have to be good at what we do, communicate it, and justify the funding."

Second, embrace technology. The future rests on providing better service, easier and faster. Decisions are made based on information, which is generated from data that is collected, stored, and analyzed. Data and information will help justify funding.

Third, emphasize training in everything. Proper training will ensure a positive response and safer conditions. Technology is constantly changing and that change impacts our equipment systems. All our employees need to stay current in their trades. Also, train and encourage all employees to be observant and to report discrepancies.

Fourth, communication is critical. Facility managers need to be effective communicators, both orally and in writing. They need to be able to sell themselves and their organization. Public relations and marketing skills are vitally important. When giving a presentation, establish a presence. Maintain eye contact—especially, with senior administrators. Speak clearly, articulate your words, and vary your tone.

Maintain a relaxed stance with natural hand movements. Be confident and smile. Be positive and relate appropriate stories. Your stories should be based on facts related to a situation. They can cultivate interest while highlighting the concept being presented, making the concept easier to understand.

Fifth, seek innovative ideas and improvements. Be open minded, listen to employee ideas and recommendations, and ask questions. Find, access, and implement best practices.

Sixth, O&M funding will continue to be a challenge. Find ways to reduce cost, expand preventive and predictive maintenance, and develop long-term partnerships with contractors and vendors.

Seventh, recognize, reward, and acknowledge employees when they deserve it. People want to be recognized for what they do. It's imperative for developing relationships. Celebrate often!

Eighth, manage by walking around (MBWA). This makes you visible to employees, and you can learn much from them. Call employees by their first name. Doing this makes employees feel that you care about them and helps build your credibility.

Ninth, respect everyone. Treat superiors, peers, employees, customers, and contractors the way you want to be treated. Don't be argumentative. Focus on patience, humility, honesty, listening actively, understanding, and empathizing with everyone. Respect helps to develop trust; in turn, trust cultivates relationships and can elevate your credibility.

Tenth, be flexible and adaptable to given situations. Know that change is constant. As a leader and manager, you must be open to new ideas and ways to address challenges.

As Frank contemplated his ten points, he recalled years earlier speaking with an employee who wanted to advance himself. Frank listened as the employee explained what he wanted to achieve. Frank told the employee he would think about it and get back to the employee with his thoughts. A few days later, the employee and Frank met; Frank offered advice on what the employee could do. The employee was gratified that Frank took the time to listen and offer ideas (the ten points) for self-improvement.

At the end of their conversation, the employee stated he appreciated the advice and would develop a plan. Five years later, Frank attended a facility management conference and bumped into the former employee. The employee was exuberant when he saw Frank. He told Frank that he had taken the advice and received his facility management certifications. He was now the deputy director of facility management at the local school system.

Managing the operations and maintenance of facilities is critically important for every organization. Facilities are becoming smarter and more sophisticated, which means facility managers also have to become smarter and better trained. They need to understand the legal, health, and safety requirements of operating and maintaining their facilities. Frank told his managers and supervisors, "Life is a journey. The road of life events is not straight. It has many twists and turns. Hopefully, we all learn from mistakes we make and the challenges we face along the way."

PART III DISCUSSION QUESTIONS

1. Why are vision, mission, goals needed in an organization?

2. How do you convert plans into action?

3. Why are organization policies and procedures necessary?

4. How should an organization go about developing and implementing a change management plan?

5. What is the purpose of vision and mission statements?

6. In what way are surveys important in a change management process?

7. Why is communication important in the change management process?

8. What is quality management and why is it important?

9. How can the FM manager ensure the department provides good quality management and customer service?

10. Why is it important for FM departments to understand the overall organization business plan?

11. Why is the FM budget always a target for reduction?

12. What is ASHRAE? Why is it important?

13. What information and tools are needed to plan effectively?

14. What are strategic, long-range, plans?

15. Why should the annual work plan be trackable from year to year?

16. Why is the department operating budget prepared for one year whereas a capital budget is multiyear?

17. What are the characteristics of the FM operating budget?

18. How do operating budget reductions negatively impact fire protection systems?

19. Why should a facility manager be involved with project inspections, punch list items, and commissioning?

20. What should FM managers do when learning of a workplace violence incident?

21. What should the FM department do when informed of an IAQ issue?

22. Why should an FM organization implement an annual report?

23. What is driving the changes and transformation within the FM profession?

APPENDICES

Appendix A
Philosophy and Style

Memorandum

To: Managers, Facilities Management Department
CC: Personnel File
From: Frank Mitchell, Director, Facilities Management
Subject: Operating and Management Philosophy

I want to take this opportunity to introduce myself and to provide you with my operating and management philosophy. I hope it will help you understand how I like to operate.

1. **Overview and Style**
    A. As the old adage goes, "If it ain't broke, don't fix it." I will ask "why" so that I will better understand the background, reasons, and logic for the way we do business. Every manager has his/her own philosophy and style. Should I be uncomfortable with the answers to my "why" questions, that will be the basis for my consideration to make appropriate changes. Rest assured I will not make changes in a vacuum.
    B. Personally, I am low-keyed and will let you do your job. I try not to be a micro-manager, but I will be when I feel it to be necessary.
    C. I support the concept of "power down" in delegating authority and responsibility. However, I will centralize when necessary.
    D. "Knowledge is power!" I obtain much of my information by wandering around, observing, and asking questions. I also want to keep up my visibility and will push to meet everyone within the organization.
    E. I am open-minded and not averse to trying something new. I welcome suggestions and positive critiques.

2. **Management Philosophy**
   A. **Awards:** I am a believer in the rewards program. I encourage you to submit awards for outstanding performance. People like to know they are doing a good job.
   B. **Access to me:** My door is always open. Anyone who wants to see me may do so. If a person has a problem, I encourage that he/she work through the supervisor and, if that does not solve the problem, come see me.
   C. **Innovation:** Be innovative! Do not keep doing something because we have always been doing it this way. Push state-of-the-art methods in your technical area. Try something new and take a risk. Learn from your mistakes. If you try something that does not work, then try something else.
   D. **Communications:** Keep me informed. I want to hear the bad news as well as good news. I do not like surprises. When you bring a problem to my attention, also give me options.
   E. **Loyalty:** I consider myself loyal to my superiors and subordinates. Likewise, I expect subordinates to be loyal to me. Do not wash "dirty linen" outside the organization. If we have a disagreement, let's begin in-house to correct it.
   F. **Counselling:** People cannot improve unless they are critiqued. I advocate counselling all personnel. Let them know how they are doing—good and bad.
   G. **Fitness:** Fitness is important for overall welfare. It has a positive impact on your outlook on life and work.
   H. **Training:** Incorporate training into everything we do. Encourage personnel to take advantage of the many different training classes and programs.
   I. **Property Accountability:** This is everyone's responsibility.
   J. **Safety:** Safety is our number one priority. That includes safety for our employees and safety for our users.
   K. **Customer Service:** As a service organization, we need to be responsive with a smile.

Appendix B
Facility Management Policies and Procedures

A separate format for policies and procedures is shown below. Below the established format is a tentative list of policies and procedures to be developed. Policies are general guidelines to address specific issues. They are important for a healthy work culture. Procedures provide instructions on how to accomplish tasks. They address who is responsible for each task and what steps need to be taken.

Policies Format

Policy Statement Number: _____________
Subject:
Date Established:
Revision Dates:
Purpose:
Policy:
Authority: Director of Facilities Management
Distribution:

Policy Codes

100: Administration and Organization
200: Work Management
300: Employee Relations
400: Professional Conduct
500: Employee Development
600: Health and Safety

Policy Code 100: Administration and Organization

- Annual Report
- Project Review Requirements
- Manager/Supervisor Leave
- Student, Casual Labor, and Temporary Employment
- Care of University Vehicles and Equipment
- Job Interviewing Policy

Policy Code 200: Work Management
- After-Hours Maintenance Response
- Use of University Credit Cards
- Identifying and Labeling Equipment
- Keys and Locks
- Preventive Maintenance
- Tool Sign Out/In

Policy Code 300: Employee Relations
- Time and Attendance
- Professional Conduct
- Dress Code

Policy Code 400: Professional Conduct
- Misappropriation of University Property
- Disciplinary Action
- Unauthorized Behavior in the Workplace

Policy Code 500: Employee Development
- Training Policy
- Lockout/Tagout Policy

Policy Code 600: Health and Safety
- Vehicle Driver Safety Policy
- Property Damage Policy
- Personal Accident or On-the-Job Injury
- Shop Safety Policy

- Chemical Hazard Communication Policy
- Mitigation and Contingency Threat Planning Policy
- Authority Having Jurisdiction Policy
- Fire Impairment Policy

Procedures Format

Procedure Number: ___________
Date Established:
Revision Dates:
Purpose:
Assigned Responsibility:
Approving Authority: Director of Facility Management
Distribution:

Procedure Codes

100: Administration
- Work Management SOP
- Removal of Abandoned Equipment
- Procedure for Refrigerant Procurement, Use, and Disposal
- Service Outage Notification Procedures
- Campus Move Requests
- Authority Having Jurisdiction

200: Building and Equipment Maintenance Procedures
- Control Valve Replacement Procedures
- Maintenance Response After Work Hours
- Building Alarm Systems Procedures and Fire Impairment
- Quality Inspection and Measurement Program
- New Equipment Inventory Report
- Preventive Maintenance Service Outage Procedure
- Preventive Maintenance Work Guidelines
- Preventive Maintenance Equipment and Structures

- Roofs
- Building Envelope (windows, doors, locks, etc.)
- Electrical Systems (lighting systems, breakers, transformers switchboards, disconnects, etc.)
- Mechanical Systems (air compressor and vacuum pumps, controls, exhaust fans and air handling units, generators)
- Plumbing Systems (drinking water systems, fixtures, piping, pumps, backflow preventers, valves, etc.)
- Fencing
- Walkways
- Trench Drains
- Air-Conditioning Schedule of Duties and Responsibilities
- Care of University Equipment
- Basic Emergency Generator and Transfer Switch Maintenance and Testing
- Parts and Materials Required to be Kept in Central Stores

300: Cleaning Services
- Cleaning Services Standard Operating Procedures
- Cleaning Equipment Standard Operating Procedures
- Infectious Disease Cleaning Plan

400: Utilities, Major Equipment, and Equipment Failure

500: Grounds and Waste Management
- Landscape and Grounds Standard Operating Procedures
- Solid Waste Management Standard Operating Procedures
- Integrated Pest Management
- Equipment Operation

600: Major Repairs and Renovations
- Project Review Procedures
- Conduct Life Cycle Analysis

700: Shop Standing Operating Procedures
- Lockout/Tagout Procedures

- Confined Space Entry Program
- Life Safety Preventive Maintenance Procedures
- Surface Cleanup and Decontamination of Blood and Body Spills
- Exterior Campus Lighting
- Slips, Trips, and Falls
- Ladder Safety
- Building and Shops Standard Operating Procedures
- Training by Trade
- Tool Sign Out/In

800: Emergency Operations Procedures

- Bomb Threat
- Chemical and Hazardous Material Spill
- Criminal Behavior
- Explosion
- Fire
- Infectious Disease Outbreak
- Medical Emergency
- Natural Disaster
  - Earthquake
  - Hurricane
  - Tornado
  - Inclement Weather Emergency (including snow)
  - Heavy Rain, Strong Wind, Lightning Activity
- Terrorism
  - Biological/Chemical Weapon Attack
  - Suspicious Activity
  - Heightened Threat Level
- Transportation Accident
  - Aircraft Accident
  - Train Accident in Surrounding Area
  - Vehicle Accident in Surrounding Area
- Utility Failure
  - Electrical Failure
  - Elevator Failure
  - Plumbing Failure

- - Steam Line Failure
  - Ventilation/HVAC Failure
- Unplanned Outage or System Malfunction
  - Natural Gas Leak
  - Emergency Equipment Shutdown
  - Disaster Recovery Procedure
  - Emergency Winterization Procedure
  - Electrical Load Shedding
- Shelter-in-Place
- Evacuation Procedure
- Emergency Closure of Facility

Appendix C
Vision, Mission, Goals

Our vision is a Facilities Management department that is:
- Customer-oriented
- Continuously emphasizing quality and improvement
- Systems-oriented
- Productive and efficient
- Environmentally conscious
- Safe in which to work
- Innovative
- Transparent

Where supervisors are:
- Accountable
- Consistent
- Fair and just
- Enthusiastic
- Ethical
- Seeking improvement
- Technically proficient
- Example-setters
- Communicating (upwards, downwards, and laterally)
- Emphasizing teamwork
- Enforcing policies and procedures
- Caring
- Teachers

Where employees are:
- Satisfied with their jobs
- Enthusiastic to come to work
- Motivated
- Friendly

- Responsive
- Valued for their skills and knowledge
- Accountable for their actions

Our mission is:

The mission of Facilities Management is to provide a building and service environment conducive to research, teaching, and comfortable living and learning, while meeting our own basic needs of well-being and growth.

Our goals and objectives are:

Goal 1: Improve the quality of customer service (internally and externally) wherein our customers are satisfied with the service they receive.

(Name of responsible individual) (Target date to complete)

Objectives:
- Develop a Facilities Management handout (electronic and brochure, handbook, service manual, etc.) to be given to each customer consisting of:
    - Organizational diagram
    - Photos of employees serving the customer
    - How to submit a work request
    - Types of work: emergency, urgent, and routine
    - How to initiate a project
    - Statistics about the organization
    - Contact information: Phone numbers, e-mails
    - Survey form

- Visit each customer and provide them with handouts.
    - Determine what is important to them
    - Have them evaluate our service

- Develop a service strategy.
  - Slogan
  - Implement an employee recognition and reward program
  - Obtain feedback to measure progress

- Develop a custodial cleaning manual and provide copy to each customer. The manual should include:
  - Schedule of cleaning
  - Definition of what is to be cleaned
  - Frequency of cleaning
  - Area to be cleaned

- Develop a custodial cleaning operations manual. Include such things as standards of cleaning, quality control, and customer feedback statistics.
- Renovate and improve FM shop space.

Goal 2: Emphasize, improve, and expand the preventive maintenance (PM) program. All shops and sections conduct PM.

(Name of responsible individual) (Target date to complete)

Objectives:
- Develop and publish a FM employee maintenance plan.
- Inventory (data plate information) all equipment in each building and create an asset database of equipment to be used for issuing PM work orders.
- Issue PM work orders to all shops and track completion.
- Conduct weekly PM meetings.
- Develop and provide monthly "tracking charts" which measure how we are doing with PM.
- Explore bar coding of equipment for PM.

Goal 3: Develop and implement a coherent and synchronized training program.

<u>(Name of responsible individual) (Target date to complete)</u>

Objectives:
- Assess employees as to their training needs. Focus on improving weaknesses. Coordinate with the Office of Personnel to assist with employee assessment and training.
- Emphasize supervisory training on policies, procedures, safety, management, and technical areas.
- Make use of vendor and supplier training at no cost.
- Explore train-the-trainer.
- Implement safety training for all shops and cleaners.

Goal 4: Scrutinize everything we do with the outlook to continuously improve.

<u>(Name of responsible individual) (Target date to complete)</u>

Objectives:
- Implement monthly performance reviews. Review objectives for the past month, discuss accomplishments and improvements.
- Review job descriptions, adjust, modify, and consider job enlargement. Coordinate with the Office of Personnel for assistance.
- Relook how we currently operate and make changes to improve what we do.
- Clean the shops, dispose of obsolete equipment and materials.
- Develop and implement PM parts kits.
  - Start with one building and collect data plate information from all equipment.
  - Decide on number of kits, which should be stocked for six months.
  - Coordinate with Procurement to order the kits.

Goal 5: Assure competent management of all Facility Management resources. This includes safety and security.

<u>(Name of responsible individual) (Target date to complete)</u>

Objectives:

- Restructure the department using existing positions.
- Expand the role of some positions.
- Fill vacant positions.
- Revise the work shift schedules.
    - As a minimum, stagger shifts to cover hours when classes are scheduled.
    - Also, cover hours when there are no classes since students reside in dormitories. This should involve only one technician. During this shift, the employee should conduct equipment checks and PM which can be tracked.
    - Implement a Duty Officer rotation of all managers. One manager is on call, after normal work hours, for one week.
- Check all electrical panel boxes, in every building, and ensure they are locked, keys are properly secured, and a policy is written.
- Evaluate overtime. Reduce where possible and track.
- Check the security of buildings. Start with dormitories since approximately 6,000 students reside in university housing, then classroom and faculty buildings.
    - Inspect and repair door locks.
    - Inspect and repair windows.
    - Clear brush and vegetation overgrowth away from buildings.
    - Verify exterior lighting is adequate. If not, add more lights.

REFERENCES

21st Century Security and CPTED: Designing for Critical Infrastructure Protection and Crime Prevention. 2nd ed. Randall I. Atlas. CRC Press: 2013.

Emergency Management for Facility and Property Managers. Richard P. Payant. McGraw-Hill Education: 2016.

Essentials of Management, 9th ed. Andrew J. DuBrin. South-Western College: 2011.

The Facility Manager's Guide to Finance and Budgeting, David Cotts and Edmund Rondeau, AMACOM: 2008

The Facility Management Handbook, 4th ed. Kathy O. Roper and Richard P. Payant. AMACOM: 2014.

Facility Manager's Maintenance Handbook. 2nd ed. Richard P. Payant and Bernard T. Lewis. McGraw-Hill: 2007.

Healthy Buildings. Dr. Joseph G. Allen and John D, Macomber, Harvard University Press, 2021.

NFPA 291: Recommended Practice for Water Flow Testing Marking of Hydrants, 2022.

NFPA 1600: National Standard on Disaster and Emergency Management and Business Continuity. National Fire Protection Association.

The Power of Habit: Why We Do What We Do in Life and Business. Charles Duhigg. Random House: 2012.

Quality Facility Management: A Marketing and Customer Service Approach.
Stormy Friday and David G. Cotts. Wiley: 1994.
In Search of Excellence: Lessons from America's Best-Run Companies. Thomas
J. Peters and Robert H. Waterman. Harper Business: 2006.

INDEX

3D printing 138

absenteeism 95

access control information 59

actuators 136

adaptable 4, 143

administration 13, 28, 71, 151, 152, 153

after-action reviews 96, 165

AHJ 61, 118

air conditioning xvii, 28, 121, 125

air handling systems 122

air pollution 165

alarm systems 59, 153

amateur radio license 61

American Society of Heating, Refrigerating, and Air Conditioning Engineers 28 *See* ASHRAE

annual budget 13, 113

annual report xii, 129, 130, 131, 140, 145, 152

annual training program 33

annual work plan (AWP) 22, 109, 110, 111, 112, 140, 145

approved equals 72

archivist 35, 71, 72

artificial intelligence (AI) 35, 135, 136

as-built drawings 58, 72

ASHRAE 28, 50, 121, 144

ASHRAE Standard 121

assessing risks 62

asset database 42, 48, 63, 159

asset life cycle 41

asset management xi, 41, 43, 44, 45, 47, 48, 50, 62, 72, 80, 86, 87

asset management database 41, 48

asset management plan 43, 44, 45, 62, 72

asset register 41

Association for Facilities Engineering (AFE) 67

Association of Higher Education Facility Officers (APPA) 67

attic stock 74

attitude xviii, xix, 86, 135, 138

audit 76, 139, 140

Authority Having Jurisdiction (AHJ). *See* AHJ 61, 118, 153

automatic door servicing 53

automation xi, 7, 44, 45, 47, 50, 86, 112, 136

AWP *See* annual work plan 111, 112, 113

baby boomers 134

barcoding 45

BAS. *See* building automation systems 50, 136

benchmarking 68, 69, 81, 82, 129

benefit-cost ratio (BCR) 110

benefits v, 13, 35, 94, 112, 121, 127

best practices 68, 69, 142

bio-digestive enzymes 76

blanket purchase orders (BPOs) 54

blood-borne pathogens 33

brainstorming 106

budget xix, 13, 22, 32, 34, 35, 48, 56, 64, 71, 73, 77, 80, 86, 109, 110, 112, 113, 116, 131, 133, 140, 141, 144, 145

build trust xiv, xviii, 4, 12, 23, 38

building automation systems (BAS) 136

building cleanliness 34

building codes xvi

building conveyance systems xvii

building information modeling (BIM) 136

building maintenance xvi

business continuity 62, 63, 64, 163

business plan 89, 109, 110, 111, 140, 144

call center. *See* WMC 29, 119

cameras 65, 137

capital budget 110, 145

capital plan 112, 140

capital projects 34, 71, 73, 81

capital replacement plan 41

cash payback 110

central database 135

central shops 7, 38, 50, 59, 76, 115

centralized database 47

certification 53, 76, 77

change management xii, 62, 93, 94, 101, 105, 144

changing habits 93

charts 8, 129, 130, 159

chemical fertilizers 137

citizen band AM radio 61

cleaning xvi, 20, 24, 34, 42, 53, 54, 76, 120, 122, 126, 137, 154, 159

clerical tasks 135

CMMS 37, 47, 48, 50, 62, 81

commissioning 74, 82, 145

commissioning agent 74

commitment 6, 45, 138

communication v, xvii, 4, 57, 59, 60, 61, 62, 82, 87, 93, 94, 95, 99, 105, 108, 133, 142, 144, 153

communication after an emergency 61

communication before an emergency 60

communication during an emergency 61

communications xv, 13, 57, 58, 59, 61, 62, 81, 86, 91, 94, 120, 126, 140, 150

community gardens 137

comparative costs 113

composting 75, 137

computer maintenance management system *See* CMMS 37, 47, 59, 81

confined space 33, 155

consider contract incentives 56

consistency 39, 79, 93, 98

construction ix, xx, 4, 6, 13, 19, 71, 72, 73, 116, 120

construction contracts 71

construction inspector 116

consultants 58

contract negotiation 56

contract specifications 73

contractors ix, xvii, 15, 21, 38, 54, 55, 56, 58, 64, 72, 90, 116, 137, 142

contracts 7, 13, 20, 21, 53, 54, 56, 71, 80, 113, 137

cooling tower water treatment 53

cost indexes 110

cost-efficient 97

counselling 126, 128, 150

CPR 33

CPTED 65, 163

credibility 3, 4, 7, 12, 15, 19, 23, 60, 93, 94, 120, 129, 142

Crime Prevention through Environmental Design. *See* CPTED 65

critical parts and materials 55

cross-training 32

culture xi, 37, 38, 39, 43, 82, 134, 151

culture change 43

custodians 24, 57, 120, 122, 125, 137

customer perception 106

customer satisfaction 91, 107

customer service xii, xiii, xv, xvii, 13, 29, 34, 43, 48, 87, 105, 106, 107, 108, 135, 136, 140, 144, 150, 158, 164

customer service evaluation form 107

customer/client violence 128

daily journal 4

damage assessment teams 64

data xvi, 45, 47, 59, 68, 111, 121, 131, 135, 136, 142, 159, 160

dedication vii, 99, 108

deferred maintenance 69, 110, 116

demand organization xvi

department goals 38

design and engineering xi, 9, 13, 71, 73, 81

design engineer 72, 115

design review 19

design standards 110

diesel fuel tanks 54

diversity 38

document archive 169

documentation 77

dream statement 98

drones 136, 137

duty officer 58, 60, 161

electric vehicles 138

electrical closets 10

electrical power failures 91

electricity xvii, 5, 137

electronic magnetic pulse (EMP) 61

elevator inspection 53

elevator maintenance 20, 53

elevators 50, 55, 59

emergencies xvi, xvii, 27, 33, 35, 42, 49, 57, 61, 62, 64, 65, 72, 90, 91, 103, 131, 133

emergency announcements 60

emergency command center 58

emergency communications 61, 91

emergency employees. *See* essential employees 103, 139

emergency generators 9, 20, 43, 54, 59

emergency management xi, xv, 20, 57, 61, 62, 63, 64, 81, 86, 87, 92, 163

emergency preparedness 33, 48

emergency procedures 28

emergency response 13, 20, 91, 133

emergency situations 54, 138

emissions 137

empathizing 142

employee assessment 34, 160

employee complaints 102

employees vii, xiv, xvii, xviii, xx, 5, 6, 7, 10, 11, 13, 20, 21, 22, 23, 24, 25, 28, 29, 31, 32, 33, 34, 35, 38, 39, 40, 48, 50, 51, 53, 55, 58, 61, 68, 71, 81, 87, 91, 94, 95, 96, 97, 98, 102, 103, 105, 107, 108, 109, 119, 126, 127, 128, 129, 130, 131, 134, 135, 136, 137, 139, 140, 141, 142, 143, 151, 158, 159

empowering employees 138

energy audit 76

energy efficiency 137

energy management xvi, 20, 135

energy usage 131, 136, 137

energy-efficient lighting 137

environment 3, 10, 75, 76, 120, 137, 158

environmental safety 95

equipment 10, 20, 22, 28, 31, 32, 37, 41, 42, 43, 44, 45, 47, 48, 49, 53, 54, 58, 59, 60, 61, 64, 72, 76, 91, 118, 122, 130, 136, 137, 138, 142, 152, 153, 154, 156, 159, 160, 161

equipment replacement 32, 130

equipment shutdown procedures 59

essential employees 103

established protocols 33

everyone has to be invested 90

Excel spreadsheets 29, 37, 47, 80

explosions 61

Facebook 61

facilitation process 97

facilitator 98

facility action plans 90

Facility Emergency Operations Center (FEOC). *See* FEOC 58

facility intelligence 49, 50, 59, 87, 118

Facility Intelligence Resource Guide (FIRG) 59

Facility Management Stakeholder Service Council (FMSSC) 140

fall protection 33

fan coil units 29

Federal Communications Commission (FCC) 61

Federal Emergency Management Agency (FEMA) 61

FEOC 58, 59, 60

filters 20, 29, 55, 77, 121

filters changed 29

financial management 141

fire alarm maintenance 32

fire alarms 118

fire code 10

fire department 61, 117

fire detection 118

fire extinguisher certification 53

fire hydrant flow testing 54

fire impairment form 118

fire plan 118

fire protection xii, 20, 28, 33, 50, 53, 54, 64, 91, 115, 116, 117, 118, 137, 140, 145, 163

fire protection control valves 118

fire pump locations 118

fire suppression 172

fire watch 118
first aid 33
first responders 51
fleet management 48
flexible 4, 39, 98, 134, 143
floor plans 136
funding xvii, 3, 8, 32, 34, 37, 48, 50, 62, 64, 68, 76, 86, 90, 110, 113, 117, 141, 142
future expansion 50, 172

garage x, 6, 7, 20, 115, 116
gasoline 138
Generation X 134
Generation Z 134
glass repair 53
global warming 137
goals xii, xvi, 3, 4, 12, 13, 20, 38, 50, 69, 80, 82, 87, 89, 90, 94, 97, 98, 101, 102, 103, 105, 107, 109, 119, 129, 130, 131, 139, 144, 157, 158
government regulations xvi
governmental agencies 58
graphs 129
grass cutting 137
grease trap cleaning 53
green chemicals 76
grounds xvi, xvii, xix, 7, 9, 13, 20, 34, 43, 45, 57, 65, 75, 94, 137, 154
growth caps 111

ham radio 61
hazardous conditions 34
hazardous materials 33, 59, 62, 91
health xiii, xvi, 28, 90, 95, 143, 151, 152

health representatives 172
health requirements 172
heating 7, 10, 13, 28, 121, 125
Hewlett-Packard 23
high-efficiency particulate air vacuums 172
high-voltage feeders 59
hiring practices 134
historical comparisons 113
honesty 99, 142
human resources 6, 28, 34, 37, 95, 98, 128
hurricane 60, 155
HVAC 7, 9, 13, 20, 21, 34, 39, 41, 50, 53, 55, 77, 102, 121, 123, 125, 126, 127, 128, 136, 137, 156

IAQ. *See* indoor air quality 119, 120, 121, 122, 123, 140, 145
identifying hazards 62
IFMA. *See* International Facility Management Association 67
implementation 43, 55, 90, 98, 103
incentive pay 102
independent authority 74
indoor air quality xii, xiii, 30, 33, 91, 102, 119, 120, 121
in-house maintenance personnel 72
infectious disease 57, 91, 136, 154, 155
informal network 126
innovation 12, 99, 135, 150
inspections 34, 48, 62, 73, 115, 117, 120, 145
insurance 112

integrated visual modelling 136

Integrated Work Management System (IWMS) 48

integrity 99

International Facility Management Association xvi, 67

Internet of Things (IoT) 136

inventory 41, 44, 48, 71, 109, 153, 159

iPad 50, 51

job descriptions 8, 23, 33, 37, 160

journal 4, 14

Just-In-Time delivery (JIT) 55

keep the boss informed 79

key performance indicators. *See* KPIs 69, 81, 107, 131

knowledge, skills, and abilities. *See* KSA 23

KPIs 69, 81, 82

KSA 23

labor 48, 80, 111, 152

landscape maintenance 20

laptop 50, 51

layoffs 102

leadership i, iii, v, vii, ix, xiii, xiv, xv, xvii, xix, 3, 4, 5, 7, 9, 11, 13, 15, 19, 21, 23, 25, 27, 29, 31, 33, 34, 35, 37, 39, 41, 43, 45, 47, 49, 50, 51, 53, 55, 57, 59, 60, 61, 63, 64, 65, 67, 68, 69, 71, 73, 75, 76, 77, 79, 81, 85, 86, 87, 89, 91, 93, 95, 97, 99, 101, 103, 105, 107, 109, 111, 113, 115, 117, 119, 120, 121, 123, 125, 127, 128, 129, 131, 133, 134, 135, 137, 139, 141, 143, 145, 149, 151, 153, 155, 157, 159, 161, 163

Leadership in Energy and Environmental Design (LEED). *See* LEED 76

LED lights 76

LEED 76, 77

LEED certification 76, 77

LEED-EBOM 76

legacy knowledge of employees 35

legal requirements xvi

lessons learned 96

liability ii

life cycle analysis 109, 154

life safety xvi, 59, 61, 118, 155

lighting 44, 50, 137, 154, 155, 161

lightning protection 63

LinkedIn 61

listening v, xv, 13, 24, 39, 93, 94, 95, 115, 142

lockout 33, 152, 154

locomotive steam whistle 60

long-range plans 110

lubrication 42

mail 24, 105, 112

maintenance x, xi, xv, xvi, xix, xx, 7, 9, 10, 11, 13, 20, 21, 24, 27, 28, 29, 30, 31, 32, 33, 34, 35, 37, 41, 42, 43, 44, 45, 47, 48, 49, 50, 53, 58, 59, 63, 65, 67, 68, 69, 71, 72, 73, 76, 77, 80, 81, 82, 85, 87, 90, 91, 94, 110, 112, 116, 120, 121, 122, 123, 126, 131, 133, 135, 142, 143, 152, 153, 154, 155, 159, 163

maintenance procedures 27, 28, 90, 153, 155

maintenance zones 7

manage by walking around. *See* MBWA xi, 12, 23, 142

management philosophy 11, 12, 82, 149, 150

marketing 87, 107, 129, 130, 140, 142, 164

mass notification system 60

master plan 22, 109, 110

MBWA 12, 23, 72, 115, 126, 128, 142

measure improvement 139

measuring xi, 67, 68, 81, 95

mechanical rooms 10

Millennials 134

minimum standards 27

mission xii, 3, 4, 20, 38, 63, 69, 80, 82, 87, 89, 90, 94, 97, 98, 101, 102, 103, 105, 120, 130, 131, 139, 144, 157, 158

mission statement 38, 82, 98, 101

mitigation strategies 62, 63, 82

monthly newsletter 95

monthly updates xii, 79

morale 32

narrative 28, 113, 129

national conferences 32

National Fire Protection Association. *See* NFPA 28, 64, 116, 117, 163

National Incident Management System (NIMS) 33, 65

natural access control 65

natural disasters 57

natural gas shutoff locations 59

natural surveillance 65

net present value (NPV) 110

newsletter x, 60, 95, 96, 106, 107

NFPA 28, 64, 116, 117, 163

NFPA 1600 64, 163

non-union 21

O&M. *See* operations and maintenance xix, 22, 32, 41, 47, 72, 73, 74, 76, 131, 135, 136, 137, 140, 142

objective 98

Occupational Safety and Health Administration (OSHA) 28

office expenses 13

office supplies 112

ongoing capital construction projects 72

ongoing construction project 72

ongoing leadership training 93

operating budget 112, 145

operating plans 90

operations and maintenance x, xv, xvi, xix, 9, 29, 32, 35, 41, 58, 68, 71, 73, 76, 80, 85, 90, 111, 120, 133, 135, 143

optical scanner 45

organization vision 98

overtime 102, 161

parking xvi, xvii, 5, 64, 108, 115

parts requisition 48

patience 49, 98, 102, 138, 142

perception xi, 37, 106

persistence 98

personnel xiii, 6, 13, 20, 28, 37, 43, 45, 54, 58, 72, 91, 107, 110, 149, 150, 160

personnel policies 6

pest control 20, 53

philosophy xii, 11, 12, 13, 82, 149, 150

physical plant xvi, 63, 64

physical safety 128, 140

physical safety and security survey 128, 140

physical security xvi, 34, 65, 87, 91

physical security threat 65

plan development 101

plan of action 3, 4, 89

planned growth 110

planned maintenance 42, 68

planning xii, xvi, xviii, 3, 12, 20, 21, 22, 32, 41, 42, 44, 45, 73, 86, 90, 93, 107, 109, 111, 112, 137, 141, 153

PM kits 44, 45

police 5, 61, 62, 65, 81, 128

policies ix, xi, xii, 6, 11, 13, 27, 28, 29, 33, 38, 43, 51, 54, 60, 61, 80, 82, 86, 87, 90, 125, 126, 128, 134, 144, 151, 157, 160

policies are guidelines 28

policy x, 12, 28, 50, 60, 61, 90, 95, 120, 121, 122, 126, 127, 151, 152, 153, 161

positive attitude xviii

postage 112

potable water xvii, 59, 91

PowerPoint 50

predictive maintenance 142

preventive maintenance (PM) xi, 13, 20, 29, 37, 41, 42, 43, 44, 45, 48, 50, 63, 80, 82, 87, 122, 131, 152, 153, 155, 159

procedures x, xi, xii, 27, 28, 29, 31, 33, 38, 43, 51, 54, 59, 60, 61, 62, 80, 82, 86, 87, 90, 111, 112, 118, 122, 125, 126, 128, 144, 151, 153, 154, 155, 157, 160

procurement xi, 53, 54, 80, 153, 160

productivity 68, 135

professionalism 39, 87, 99

Program Budget Advisory Committee (PBAC) 112

progressive discipline 125, 126, 127

project management 48

property management xv, xvi, xvii

property protection xvi

public relations 142

public safety 31, 95

public works x, xvi, xvii, xx, 133, 137, 141

punch list 73, 145

purchase orders (POs) 54,166

quality management xii, xv, xvii, 37, 43, 48, 67, 69, 87, 91, 105, 106, 108, 135, 136, 140, 144

quality of service 69, 106

Radio Amateur Civil Emergency Service (RACES) 61

reactive maintenance 32, 68, 69

recalibration 42

record drawings 58, 71

recycling xvi, 7, 13, 20, 75, 134, 137

renovation ix, xx, 13, 19, 120

repairs 35, 42, 47, 63, 154

replacement of parts 42

Report to the Nation on Workplace Violence 128

requests for proposals (RFP) 55

respect xviii, 39, 99, 135, 142

restrooms xvii, 136

return on investment (ROI) 110

review process 102

risk insurer 118

risk management 28, 95

robotic floor scrubbers 137

robotic grass mowers 137

roofs 13, 63, 154

safety xvi, 13, 28, 31, 32, 33, 34, 45, 59, 61, 64, 90, 95, 116, 118, 125, 127, 128, 140, 143, 150, 151, 152, 155, 160

safety codes 33

safety practices 32

safety representatives 90

safety requirements 143

salaries 13, 112

sanitary sewer jetting 53

sanitary systems xvii

satellite phones 58, 61

save energy 136

scope of work (SOW) 54

scuppers 63

security xvi, xvii, 34, 60, 64, 65, 87, 91, 125, 127, 128, 136, 140, 160, 161, 163

sensors 136

service xii, xiii, xv, xvii, 13, 15, 20, 29, 34, 43, 48, 53, 54, 55, 57, 60, 61, 64, 67, 69, 80, 86, 87, 95, 97, 99, 105, 106, 107, 108, 113, 131, 134, 135, 136, 137, 140, 142, 144, 150, 153, 158, 159, 164

service contracts 13, 20, 54, 80, 113

service-level agreement 54, 55

sexual harassment 33

share the wealth mentality 32

shelter in place 33

smart sensors 136

smartphones 136

smile xviii, 6, 24, 142, 150

snow xvii, 54, 57, 91, 155

soil 49, 137

solar panels 76, 138

solid waste xvi, xvii, 7, 13, 20, 53, 134, 137, 154

space management xvi

special occasion letters 25

specialty service contractors 54

staff meetings 19

stages of resistance 93

stakeholders xiii, xiv, 90, 95, 96, 103, 107, 129

standard operating procedures 59, 62, 80, 154, 155

standard unit costs 113

standardization 111

stewardship 99

storm preparedness 91

storm water sand filter cleaning 53

strategic planning 41, 90, 109

strike plan 21, 80

style v, xii, 12, 13, 149

substitution 72

surveillance 65, 136, 176

survey 29, 95, 128, 140, 158, 170, 177

sustainability xi, xiii, xvi, 48, 75, 76, 77, 81, 110, 131, 135, 136, 137

SWOT analysis 20

system upgrades 50

tactical plans. *See* mid-range planning 110

tagout 33, 152, 154

tax law 110

teamwork 99, 135, 157

technology xvi, xvii, 7, 8, 12, 32, 34, 35, 47, 48, 51, 59, 61, 93, 130, 133, 134, 135, 136, 137, 142

telecommunications 112

termination 127

territorial reinforcement 65

terrorism 91, 155

timeline 94, 98

tolerance 135

tornado 60, 155

town hall meetings 93, 95

trailer-mounted generators 60

training xi, xvii, xx, 4, 8, 13, 22, 28, 31, 32, 33, 34, 35, 50, 51, 62, 74, 76, 80, 81, 86, 87, 90, 93, 107, 108, 118, 121, 126, 128, 134, 135, 137, 141, 142, 150, 152, 155, 159, 160

training based on job descriptions 33

training schedule 32

training videotaped 74

transportation xvi, 55, 64, 155

trash. *See* solid waste xvii, 24

trust. *See* build trust xiv, xviii, 4, 7, 12, 13, 15, 23, 24, 38, 39, 59, 60, 86, 93, 94, 142

turnover 34, 72

Twitter 61

U.S. Green Building Council 76

underground storage tanks 59

uniforms 39, 112

union 21, 37, 80, 90, 95, 101, 102, 103

union representatives 95, 101, 103

unit cost comparison 113

utilities 13, 41, 60, 71, 112, 154

utility cost per square foot 68

values 38, 89, 94, 98, 99, 102, 130, 134

variances 113

vendors ix, xvii, 34, 38, 53, 55, 56, 58, 60, 137, 142

ventilation 7, 10, 13, 119, 121, 125, 156

vision xii, 20, 38, 80, 82, 86, 87, 89, 90, 94, 97, 98, 101, 102, 103, 105, 130, 131, 139, 144, 157

volatile organic compounds (VOC) 122

warranties 71

water disruption 91, 92

water treatment 20, 34, 53, 91, 137

water valve locations 59

weather emergencies 33

windows 63, 119, 154, 161

WMC 58, 119

work orders 29, 47, 48, 51, 80, 102, 130, 159

work requests 29, 80, 93, 108, 119, 121

work shifts 102

workforce productivity 68

workplace violence xii, 33, 91, 125, 128, 140, 145

written policies and procedures 27

YouTube 34, 108

ABOUT THE AUTHOR

Dr. Richard Payant spent more than 22 years as Director of Facilities Management at a major university, and 23 years with the U.S. Army Corps of Engineers. He has established and directed operations and maintenance programs and environmental management programs. He now teaches in the George Mason University Facility Management certificate program.

www.ingramcontent.com/pod-product-compliance
Lightning Source LLC
Chambersburg PA
CBHW060918140726
47996CB00001B/298